Special Education: Plain and Simple

A Quick Guide

for Parents, Teachers, Advocates,

Attorneys and Others

PATRICIA L. JOHNSON HOWEY, B.A., I.R.P.

BEYOND THE SUNSET PUBLISHERS

Westpoint, Indiana 47992

Special Education: Plain and Simple

By Patricia L. Johnson Howey

Published using Dyslexie Font

Printed in the United States of America

Library of Congress Cataloging-in-Publication Data

Library of Congress Control Number: 2021910689

Johnson Howey, Patricia L

Special Education - Plain and Simple, 2nd Edition

ISBN 13: 978-0-578-90057-5

1. Education

2. Law

Using this Book

The information and legal citations in this book provide a broad overview of the topics and may or may not include the most up-to-date information about the law and special education. Legal citations are included for the reader's convenience. Not all citations are included for every topic.

Keeping this book short, simple, and easy to read means not all special education topics are addressed. Many are intentionally omitted. The book does not address early intervention for infants and toddlers and special education preschool, and many other worthy topics.

We strongly suggest you consult with a special education attorney in your state or contact your state's Department of Education for information about topics not covered, up-to-date information, legal advice, and information specific to your state.

The "e-book" version of this book includes embedded links that take you directly to specific information to locations in the book or to websites on the internet.

Acknowledgments

We wish to acknowledge the following individuals who reviewed sections of the manuscript and provided valuable suggestions and ideas. This book would not exist without their help and advice!

Jacob (Jake) Burton: Indiana teacher, coach, Tippecanoe School Corporation Board Trustee, and former school administrator. Thank you for reviewing certain chapters and suggesting edits. Your perspective as an educator is invaluable.

Jim Comstock-Galagan, J.D.: Retired Louisiana civil rights and special education attorney and faculty member of the College of William and Mary's Institute of Special Education Advocacy. Thank you for your expertise and help with the chapters on Due Process and Alternative Dispute Resolution.

Kerry Davis: I cannot thank you enough for taking time out of your busy life to review sections of the manuscript and offering suggestions for improvement.

Paula Guzzo: Retired Indiana InSource Parent Resource Advocate and mother of Scott. Thank you for reading and critiquing sections of the manuscript.

Carl Hale, Ph.D., Indiana Neuropsychologist. Your help with the evaluation and reevaluation sections allows these parts to be much more "parent-friendly." Thank you, and God bless.

Dianna Harper, M.S.: Alabama special education teacher, psychometrist, and daughter of my best friend throughout elementary and high school. Thank you for giving a teacher's perspective on the manuscript.

Dorene Philpot, J.D.: Texas special education parent attorney and author of the following books: "Do-It-Yourself Special Education Due Process: An Educational Guide" and "I Can't Make This Stuff Up — Special Education Funnies, Foibles & Embarrassments." Your expertise from your former life as a journalist was invaluable in improving this book.

Mandy Rogers, B.S.N.: Mississippi parent, a long-time advocate for parents, and mother of Nathan and Ben. "I can think of no mother more deserving than a mother who had to give one back." Erma Bombeck.

Wayne Steedman, J.D.: Maryland special education parent attorney and Wrightslaw presenter. Wayne read and edited sections of the manuscript and offered suggestions from the legal perspective. Thank you so much!

Shari Watson: Colorado special education parent advocate. You never hesitate to help in any way. I appreciate that you immediately agreed to review sections of the manuscript and offered advice and suggestions on helping make it more reader-friendly. I cannot thank you enough!

x

Dedication

This Book is Dedicated to:

Jodie, Roger, Kerry, and Tiffany — the most important teachers in my life.

The memory of **Kayla Bower** — who taught me more about ethics in an hour than I could have learned from hundreds of hours of legal ethics classes.

The memory of **George and Stony Early** — the pioneers of special education who first introduced me to disabilities and the non-existent world of special education in the 1960s.

The memory of **Jordan Hicks** – whose untimely death at the age of 20, taught me how little control I actually have over life.

The memory of **Walter Johnson**, my grandfather and moral compass - whose advice taught me to always be true to myself.

Connie Freeman, Bette Rubinstein, and **Cathy Young** — the first parents I met when I began my special education journey. They became my mentors and supporters. They remain my good friends to this day.

Jim Comstock-Galagan — who taught me to use context and reason instead of argument and debate to get better special education services for children!

Stan Miller — who taught me to love the law and represented our family throughout three years of a due process hearing and federal court case.

Jimi Carter Miller — Mother of three sons with disabilities, who also made the ultimate sacrifice of having to "give one back."

Pete and Pam Wright - who gave me a national campus for advocacy training and offered moral support and encouragement during the long process of writing this book.

Table of Contents

Introduction

> My mother told me two things constantly. One was to be a lady and the other was to be independent, and the law was something most unusual for those times because for most girls growing up in the '40s, the most important degree was not your B.A. but your M.R.S. – Ruth Bader Ginsburg

Congratulations! Reading this book means you are taking the first important step toward learning about or refreshing your memory on special education.

The eleven lessons in this book focus on the most important things you need to know. Included are an overview of the laws and your rights as a parent of a child with a disability.

Warning: Learning about the law is like trying to herd cats. The target is always moving!

When you go on a trip, it is helpful to have a map, an atlas, or a **GPS**. This book is your guide as you venture through the world of special education.

Information is arranged so it can be found quickly. You don't need to read it from cover to cover. Each lesson stands on its own. Included are links to related or more advanced information in the book or on the internet.

Reading this book will give you a basic understanding of special education. More importantly, the lessons offer a firm foundation on which you can continue to build your knowledge.

This book is also useful to brush up on, refresh your memory about special education, or review what you have learned.

This Book is for You!

Are you new to special education and looking for easy-to-understand information? Are you overwhelmed by "legalese?" If so, this book is for you!

Parents of children with disabilities often do not have the time and energy to read a long book. This is especially true for those still in shock at learning of their child's disability.

The author attempts to make the complex subject of special education as plain and simple as possible. Each lesson gives an overview of special education topics. Most people can finish each lesson in an hour or less.

Not everyone who reads this book is new to special education. Perhaps you are an advocate, attorney, law student, teacher, related service provider, paraprofessional, or psychologist who already knows the basics of special education.

Not to worry! In each lesson are information, links, and citations to more advanced legal issues.

Many books have been written on special education. Several of my favorites are authored by Peter W.D. Wright and Pamela Darr Wright. The Appendix lists their works and other books by experts in the field and many other resources.

So, let's get started!

LESSON ONE: Getting Started

"Would you tell me please, which way I ought to go from here?"

"That depends a good deal on where you want to get to."

"I don't much care where - "

"Then it doesn't matter which way you go." - Lewis Carroll, Alice in Wonderland

So, which way do you go from here?

In special education, it really does matter!

The Law

Yes, Alice, there are laws about special education. This lesson refers to the federal law, the Individuals with Disabilities Education Act (IDEA).

The IDEA statute is at 20 U.S.C. §1400, and its Regulations are at 34 C.F.R. Part 300.

This lesson will also introduce you to the "Commentary." You will learn more about the Commentary in Lesson Two.

Most states also have their own special education laws. You can find your state's laws and regulations at the Law Librarians' Society of Washington, DC website. The Appendix includes a link to this website.

Lesson Two includes in-depth information about special

education law and other laws that affect special education.

Special Education

Special education is "specially designed instruction, offered at no cost to parents that meets the unique needs of a "child with a disability."

A "child with a disability" is defined as one who needs special education and related services because of the disability.

"At no cost" means you cannot be charged for special education and related services. You will have to pay the same fees as other parents for regular education items and services.

It may help to think of special education this way: Public schools must teach students with a wide range of abilities. Most children can learn from the regular class material and can adjust to different teaching methods.

Children with disabilities often cannot do this. They learn in different ways than the typical student. They need "specially designed instruction." Sometimes, that is the only way they can learn. Specially designed instruction is what makes special education "special!"

Your school must provide a free appropriate public education (FAPE) designed to meet your child's unique needs. Specially designed instruction is an essential part of a FAPE.

The legal definitions for many of the terms in this lesson are at 34 C.F.R. §§300.4 – 300.45.

Specially Designed Instruction

"Specially designed instruction" is changing the content, methodology, or delivery of instruction as necessary to meet a child's unique needs. This includes being able to access the general education curriculum.

Your child must have the same chance to meet the educational standards expected of children without disabilities. Schools must give children with disabilities a chance to be in general education classes, nonacademic programs, and extracurricular activities.

If needed, your school must provide supplementary aids and services to allow your child to be involved in these programs, classes, and activities. You will learn more about this in Lesson Eight.

Specially designed instruction can occur in a classroom, in your home, in hospitals, institutions, and other settings. It includes physical education (PE), travel training, and vocational education.

Travel Training is instruction for children with significant intellectual disabilities or other disabilities. It teaches skills a child needs to move from place to place in and about the school, home, work, and the community. Travel Training is also available to other children who need to how to navigate their environment.

Vocational education is an organized program that prepares children for careers that do not need a college degree.

PE includes physical and motor fitness, motor skills and patterns, aquatics and dance, individual and group games, movement education, motor development, and sports.

Suppose your child cannot be in regular PE. In that case, your school must design an Adapted Physical Education (APE) program or provide a special PE program. You will learn more about PE in Lesson Eight.

Special education and related services must meet all your state's academic standards and legal requirements.

Special education is provided through an Individualized

Education Program (IEP). The IEP is the plan that spells out your child's specially designed instruction and all other services and supports. You will learn more about the IEP in Lesson Seven.

Eligible children with disabilities in preschool, elementary school, and/or high school must receive a free appropriate public education (FAPE).

Legal definitions for many of these terms are at 34 C.F.R. §§300.4 – 300.45 and 300.101.

One Size Fits All Doesn't Fit Anyone Very Well!

A "One Size Fits All" (OSFA) special education program is not specially designed instruction. OSFA programs are designed to be convenient for schools.

How do you recognize an OSFA program? One way is if your school says it has a special program for "all children with autism" or "all children with learning disabilities."

Children are like snowflakes; no two are alike. Their needs are unique, even when they have the same diagnosis, disability, or are in the same disability category. Placing a child in a classroom because of a label is not "specially designed instruction."

More information about "OSFA" programs is in the Commentary, FR, Vol. 71, No. 156, 46587 (2006).

As the parent of an eligible special education child, you are an equal member of a group called the "IEP team." This team designs and carries out almost every aspect of your child's education. You will learn more about the IEP team in Lesson Seven.

Getting Into Special Education

At this point, you may be asking, "What do I do to get specially designed instruction for my child?" The short answer is, "Nothing." The realistic answer is different.

Schools must find, evaluate, and identify all children with disabilities between the ages of 3 and 21 who live inside its boundaries. This is called "Child Find." You will learn more about this in Lesson Four.

While the legal answer is you need not do anything to get your child into special education, often parents must help a school "find" their child.

More information about Child Find is at 34 C.F.R. §§300.111, 300.131, and 300.134 and in the *Commentary*, FR Vol. 71, No. 156, 46727, (2006).

Referral

To receive special education, someone must first refer a child for an initial evaluation. This must be a full, individualized evaluation (FIE). You must give written consent before your school can evaluate your child.

An evaluator will administer tests to your child. When the testing is finished, you and the IEP team will look at the test results and other available information. This team will decide whether your child has a disability and, if so, whether he or she needs special education and related services.

The information from the FIE suggests whether the child appears to have a disability and the type of instruction, related services, and other supports that are needed. You will learn more about the FIE in Lesson Four.

You, your state Department of Education (DOE), or someone from your school can refer a child for an initial evaluation. You will learn more about the referral process in Lesson Four.

More information about the referral process and initial evaluations is at 34 C.F.R. §300.301 – 300.305 and in the *Commentary*, FR, Vol. 71, No. 156, 46656, 46727, 46750 (2006).

Deadlines and Timelines

Almost everything in special education has a deadline. A deadline is a specific time when something must be finished.

Most deadlines are referred to as "days." This term means a school must do something within a certain number of days. Most deadlines are timelines schools must follow. But some deadlines are for you. Each lesson will explain any deadlines that apply to the topics found there.

What is a "Day?"

When you read about timelines and deadlines, it is essential to know what the word "day" means. "Day" can mean different things, even when the term is used within the same law.

A "day" can mean a calendar day, a business day, a school day, an instructional day, or an administrative day. When you see the words "day" or "days," look for a definition that explains the word's meaning.

Unless the law says differently, "day" or "days" means calendar days.

Many times, definitions are found in the beginning section of a law. However, sometimes they will be scattered throughout.

The definition of "day," "business day," and "school day" is at 34 C.F.R. §300.11.

If you remember only one thing from this Lesson, remember this: a "One Size Fits All" (OSFA) program is not specially designed instruction.

Lesson Summary

In this lesson, you began your journey into the world of special education. You learned about "Child Find," "days," "deadlines and timelines," "special education," "FIE's," "specially designed instruction", and "referral." Next you will learn about the IDEA and other laws that affect special education.

LESSON TWO: The Law

> *A law is valuable, not because it is a law, but because there is a right in it. - Henry Ward Beecher*

Learning About the Law

Experienced parent advocates know a good understanding of the law is essential. This lesson is your introduction to several of these laws. You can continue building on what you learn here.

The first thing to remember is laws are moving targets, changing from day to day. From the minute you pick up this book until you finish reading it, there will have been changes in laws.

State complaints, due process hearing decisions, and court decisions are continually explaining the law. Learning to read and understand these decisions will help you know what the law means in different situations, conditions, and locations.

Every so often, Congress amends the federal law. As you read this book, Congress is looking at amending the IDEA for the fifth time. You must always try to keep up with any amendments. They affect your and your child's rights and the special education programs.

Don't get discouraged if you are not always up to date on changes in the laws. Even attorneys have a hard time doing so! Just do your best.

This lesson will not include decisions and court opinions. They change too often for any book have the most recent information.

The Appendix has resources to help you keep up to date on changes in the law and court decisions. Included also are links to free legal research tools.

Individuals with Disabilities Education Act (IDEA)

The most important law for you to know about is the IDEA. Passed by Congress in 1975, it controls and funds special education in all states and U.S. Territories.

Before 1975, most children with disabilities were not allowed to go to school. More than one million were excluded entirely from getting a public education.

When Congress passed the first special education law, it was called the Education of All Handicapped Children Act (EAHCA). Its focus was on access. It opened the schoolhouse door to public education for children with disabilities.

Congress made significant changes to the EAHCA in 1983, 1990, 1997, and 2004. Some experts think Congress will amend it again soon.

In 2004, Congress changed the law's name to the Individuals with Disabilities Education Improvement Act (IDEA).

When reading the law, it is essential to understand the meaning of "must" and "shall." Either of these words means something is required. They are not suggestions or options. The *Commentary*, FR, Vol. 71, No. 156, 46666 (2006)

The process for making special education law begins when Congress passes a statute. The

IDEA is the statute that sets the standards for special education.

The U.S. Department of Education (USDOE) then writes regulations. These carry out, explain, and clarify the statute.

Both the statute and regulations are "the law." The IDEA statute is at 20 U.S.C. §§1400–1419, and the regulations are at 34 C.F.R. Part 300.

If your state has passed a special education law, you can find it at the Law Librarians' Society of Washington, DC. The Appendix includes a link to its website.

You and your child have rights, protections, and safeguards under the IDEA and its regulations. You will learn more about this in Lesson Three.

Purposes of the IDEA

The most important part of the IDEA and the regulations is the section called "Purposes."

One of the purposes of the IDEA is to give children with disabilities an education to prepare them: (1) to go on to college or some other type of training; (2) to find and keep a job; and (3) to live as an adult as independently as possible.

In 2004, when Congress changed the IDEA, it found children with disabilities had received access to public education. But it noted that the expectations had been set too low for children with disabilities. Teachers were also not using scientifically based methods when teaching them.

The purposes of this title are — to ensure that all children with disabilities have available to them a free appropriate public education that emphasizes special education and related services designed to meet their unique needs and prepare them for further education, employment, and independent living. 20 U.S.C. §1400(d)(1).

Because of low expectations and teachers not using proper teaching methods, the outcomes for special education students were dismal. Too many were not functional and self-sufficient adults who had homes, jobs, and friends.

Congress changed the focus of the IDEA to improve special education outcomes. Now, schools must have high expectations for students in special education. They must also use better teaching methods with scientific-based instructional methods.

Section 504 of the Rehabilitation Act

Section 504 is a federal civil rights law that affects the education of children with disabilities. It was the first disability civil rights law ever enacted.

Section 504 protects against discrimination based on disability. It gives children with disabilities equal access to schools. This access includes academics, non-academics, and extracurricular activities.

No otherwise qualified individual with a disability in the United States, as defined in §705(20) of this title, shall, solely by reason of her or his disability, be excluded from the participation in, be denied the benefits of, or be subjected to discrimination under any program or activity receiving Federal financial assistance ... 29 U.S.C. §794(a)

The Section 504 statute is at 29 U.S.C. §794, and its Regulations are at 34 C.F.R. Part 104. The section that applies to preschool, elementary, and secondary education is at Subpart D.

Compared to the IDEA, Section 504 gives broad protection to people with disabilities and those who advocate for them. Some call it an "umbrella" law because it covers many more people. But it also has fewer rights and protections.

You can see the difference between Section 504's Procedural Safeguards at 34 C.F.R. §104.36 with the IDEA's Procedural Safeguards at 34 C.F.R. §§300.121 and 300.500 – 300.520.

Section 504 applies only to programs and activities that receive federal funding in every state and U.S. Territory. It covers colleges, public schools, charter schools, and some private schools.

Unlike the IDEA, schools receive no funding under Section 504 because it is a civil rights law.

Both the IDEA and Section 504 give children with disabilities a right to a FAPE. The definition under each law is very different.

FAPE under Section 504 means *equal access*. Schools that "meet the needs of a child with a disability as adequately as it meets the needs of nondisabled students" have provided a FAPE.

Section 504 defines a FAPE at 34 C.F.R. §104.33, and the definition of a FAPE in IDEA is at 34 C.F.R. 300.17.

As you continue to study the laws, you will begin to better understand the differences between Section 504 and the IDEA. Table 1 shows a few of these examples.

Table 1

IDEA	SECTION 504
Right to FAPE that meets child's unique needs and prepares them for further education, employment, and independent living. Includes academics, non-academics, athletics, extracurricular activities. Provides rights and protections for students and parents.	Bans disability-based discrimination, bullying, harassment in programs or activities receiving federal funding. Provides equal opportunity to take part in academics, athletics, extracurricular activities.
Applies to public schools, public school districts, public charter schools, and magnet schools.	Applies to public schools, public school districts, public charter schools, magnet schools, colleges, states, public or private agencies, institutions, organizations, persons, and other entities that receive federal funding directly or through another recipient.
The disability must adversely affect educational performance and, by reason thereof, the child must need special education and related services.	Physical or mental impairment of a major bodily function that substantially limits one or more major life activities. Includes activities or functions not specifically listed. Disability does not need to adversely affect educational performance.
Applies to ages 3-21 or longer in some states.	Applies to preschool, elementary, and secondary education programs. Students must be of the age when schools provide educational services to the nondisabled, when state law requires educational services, or when a state provides FAPE under the IDEA.
Child Find provision.	Child Find provision differs from the IDEA.

Requires an initial, comprehensive, individual evaluation. Allows for IEE. Requires triennial reevaluations unless the parent and school agree otherwise. Requires reevaluation before a change in eligibility.	Must evaluate only upon parent request. Formal testing is not required. No provision for IEE. Requires periodic reevaluations. Requires reevaluation before a significant change of placement or exiting from a 504 plan.
Parental consent is required for initial evaluation, reevaluation, provision of services.	Parental consent is required only for initial evaluation. Parental notice only for the provision of services.
Requires parent participation.	Requires notice only.
Substantial rights and safeguards, including the right to hearing and appeal process with extensive procedures and independent adjudicator.	Requires notice and copy of procedural safeguards. Right to hearing and review process developed by the school.
Requires written IEP with parent participation and placement based on IEP.	Does not require a written plan. School decides whether the parent is a team member. Placement is not necessarily based on a 504 plan.
Entitled to FAPE during suspensions, expulsions.	Entitled to FAPE during suspensions/expulsions only if a behavior is linked to disability.

Family Education Rights and Privacy Act

The Family Education Rights and Privacy Act (FERPA) is a federal law that protects the privacy and confidentiality of educational records for *all parents and students*. It is not limited to special education students.

FERPA requirements are incorporated into the IDEA. For your convenience, citations to both laws are included in this lesson.

Information about FERPA is at 34 C.F.R. Part 99.

Your child's educational records are private. With few exceptions, they cannot be released without your consent or your child's consent if your child is 18 years old.

Your school can release "directory" information without your permission unless you or your adult child tells it not to do so.

Examples of directory information are participation in extracurricular and athletic activities, degrees and awards, and fields of study.

Education records include documents your school keeps about your child no matter how they are stored. Records can be handwritten or printed, kept electronically, or on computer media. They can be emails, text messages, video or audio tape, film, microfilm, or microfiche.

If someone from school keeps personal notes about your child and doesn't share them with anyone else, they are not educational records. However, once that person shares the notes

with *anyone else*, they become educational records.

You or your child can look at school records or give someone else permission to look at them.

Your school must allow you to look at the educational records "without unnecessary delay" and before an IEP meeting, a resolution meeting, or a hearing.

You will learn more about resolution meetings and hearings in Lesson Eleven.

In no case can a school delay parent access to records for more than 45 days. FERPA does not define "day," so the term means calendar days.

Once you ask to see your child's records, your school can't tamper with or destroy them.

More information about education records is at the IDEA regulations, 34 C.F.R. §300.613, and the FERPA regulations at 34 C.F.R. Part 99.

FERPA does not say how long a school must keep education records. However, the IDEA requires schools to keep them until they are no longer needed for school services.

Parents must be notified before a school destroys a child's special education records. More information about this is at 34 C.F.R. §300.624.

Educational records may be kept in several different places. Your school must give you a list of where it keeps your child's records if you ask for it.

More information about where school records are kept is at 34 C.F.R. §300.616.

Your school may charge for copies of records unless it prevents a parent from reviewing them. Schools cannot charge you a fee to search for or collect school records. More information about this is at 34 C.F.R. §300.617.

If your child's records are incorrect or inaccurate, you can ask for a correction. If your school refuses, you can ask for a hearing or write a letter saying why the records are incorrect.

If your school does not obey FERPA or the IDEA, you can file a written complaint. You will learn more about complaints in Lesson Three and hearings in Lesson Eleven.

You should look at your child's records at least once a year. A good time to do this is before each school year ends. Some schools destroy certain school records at the end of each year.

There are other times you should look at the records. Planning a move to another school district or changing schools are times for you to review records. When your child changes schools, is graduating, aging out, or otherwise leaving school, you should get copies of all educational records.

Make sure you have copies of all records your child might need to qualify for adult services. Colleges, trade schools, Vocational Rehabilitation, and Social Security disability services may ask to see these records.

The Commentary

This lesson would not be complete without telling you about the "*Commentary*." It is not a law, but it has information that can be especially useful.

You can find the *Commentary* at the Federal Register, Volume 71, No. 156, pages 46540-46845, published on August 14, 2006.

The Wrightslaw website has a searchable pdf file that you can download, save, or print. The Appendix has a link to this website.

After Congress amended the IDEA statute in 2004, the USDOE wrote proposed regulations. Members of the public had a chance to read and comment on them.

The USDOE studied the comments, replied to many of them, and made changes to the proposed regulations based on the comments. These were published in the Federal Register as an "Analysis of Comments and Changes," or "the *Commentary*."

Often, answers about the IDEA can be found only in the *Commentary*. Some courts have used the *Commentary* to explain their special education rulings. See: *Ty v. New York Dept. of Educ.*, 584 F.3d 412 (2009), and *Sheils v Pennsbury Sch. Dist.*, Civil Action No. 14-2736, US Dist. Ct. Pa., Mem. Op. (2015).

You can find both decisions by using *Google Scholar.*

Your State's Law

Many state legislatures also adopted their own special education laws. Some state laws simply adopt the **IDEA** word for word. Other states expand on the **IDEA** requirements. Special education state laws must give parents at least the same rights they have under the **IDEA**.

You can compare your state law with the **IDEA** to see if it gives you more rights.

You need to understand your state's laws and the **IDEA**.

If you cannot find your state law, ask your **DOE** to send you a copy.

If you remember only one thing from this lesson, remember this: Your school must prepare your child for further education, employment, and independent living!

Lesson Summary

In this lesson you learned about the **IDEA**, Section 504, **FERPA**, and the *Commentary*. Next you will learn about your procedural rights and safeguards.

LESSON THREE: Rights and Safeguards

> I believe that every right implies a responsibility; every opportunity an obligation; every possession, a duty. – John D. Rockefeller

Your Rights

Imagine a world where all students leave school fully prepared for "further education, employment, and independent living!" That means much more than just earning a diploma.

An appropriate education prepares a child for life outside of a classroom. If children with disabilities do not learn the skills they need to be successful adults, a diploma has no value.

The IDEA gives you and your child many rights and protections. If you look at special education law, there is one word that stands out over and over. That word is "Parent."

Did you know the words "Parent" or "Parents" are included in the IDEA statute at least 339 times? Congress must have believed you had an essential role in your child's education to use those words so often.

Maybe it is because you are the one person who is always there for your child. You send your child off to school in the morning. You are there when they get home. You provide stability in your child's world.

Clearly, Congress understands how important you are to your child's education. It gave you a seat at the IEP table and made you an equal member of the team that makes decisions.

Change is the norm in school. Many children have a different teacher every year. Principals get promoted, move to other positions, or retire. IEP teams have new members every year. Sometimes schools close, and your child must go to a new campus.

Congress knows this and wants your child to have one thing that stays the same. That is why you are an essential team member who helps make decisions about your child's education.

The IDEA gives you great power and many rights but few responsibilities. If you wanted to, you could drop your child off at preschool and pick him or her up after high school. Other than making sure your child is in school, the law doesn't require much else of you.

Taking the time to read this book says a lot about you. Clearly, you want your child to become a successful adult. You are willing to do what it takes to see your child is prepared.

Perhaps your goal is for your child to go on to school or get vocational training after high school. You know how important it is to learn the skills to find and keep a job and to live as independently as possible as an adult.

If so, it does not matter that the law requires little of you. If you want your child to be a successful adult, you have huge responsibilities. You are getting off to a great start by learning about special education!

Notice of Procedural Safeguards

Do you remember your first special education experience? You were invited to a meeting. When you got there, the room was full of people. Some you knew. Others were complete strangers.

You were given a long document printed in tiny letters and asked if you had any questions. Maybe someone asked if they should read it to you.

Like many parents, you may have felt alone and afraid. You were expecting a Parent/Teacher conference. This meeting was nothing like that!

At the time, you may not have known the importance of the document you received. It was your Notice of Procedural Safeguards (NOPS). It explains your and your child's rights and protections under the IDEA.

The NOPS tells you what to expect and what to do when you disagree. It also gives important information about deadlines and the special education process.

Schools must give parents a copy of the NOPS at least once a year and at certain other times. When these times are is found in the NOPS.

Sadly, the size of the NOPS frightens many parents, and they never read it. Some parents are too ashamed to admit they cannot read well enough to understand it. Even parents who read well can find it hard to know what all the information in the NOPS means.

The NOPS is a legal document, so it is not easy to read. Too many parents never know all their rights and safeguards because they cannot understand the NOPS.

The remaining lessons in this book will help you learn more about your rights and protections. This lesson is your Reader's Digest© version of the NOPS. For now, just remember all your rights can fit into four broad areas.

More information about the **NOPS** is at 34 **C.F.R.** §300.504 and 34 **C.F.R.** §§300.121 and 300.500 – 300.520. The *Commentary* also contains many references to the **NOPS** procedural safeguards.

Right Number One: To Be Involved.

Your school must invite you to all **IEP** and placement meetings. If you cannot attend an **IEP** meeting in person, your school must arrange for you to participate in another way. It can change the date or time of the meeting or let you attend by telephone, video conference, other electronic means, or in some other way.

Your school must invite you to take part in all decisions about your child's education. It must get your permission – or at least give you a chance to disagree – before it can make nearly any decision that affects your child.

You must give written voluntary consent before your school can evaluate, reevaluate, place your child in special education, or begins special education services for the first time.

Schools must make sure parents understand everything to which they are being asked to consent and that they know they can withdraw consent at any time.

More information about Consent is at 34 **C.F.R.** §300.9, §300.300, §300.622 and in the Commentary, FR, Vol. 71, No. 156, 46551, 46585, 46588, 46592, 46593, 46597, 46603, 46604, 46608, 46626, 46629 – 46643, 46658 – 46660, 46669 – 46670, 46672 – 46676, 46681 – 46682, 46685 – 46687, 46690 – 46691, 46727 – 46728 (2006).

Your child's program and placement cannot be changed, nor can your child be removed from special education without giving you a chance to disagree. There are several ways for you to do this. You will learn more about due process in Lesson Eleven.

You are an equal member of the IEP team. You have the same say as anyone else. Your school must allow you to help in planning the IEP and deciding your child's placement. You can invite other people to the IEP meetings. You will learn more about the IEP team in Lesson Seven.

More information about parents as IEP team members is at 34 C.F.R. §§300.23, 300.116, 300.321, and 300.328, and in the *Commentary*, FR, Vol. 71, No. 156, 46669 – 46670, 46673, 46688 (2006).

If you or your child have a disability or your native language is other than English, and you need an interpreter, your school must provide one.

More information about the right to an interpreter is at 34 C.F.R. §§300.29, 300.322(d) and (e), and in the Commentary, FR, Vol. 71, No. 156, 46564, 46570, 46572, 46679, 46688 (2006).

If you ask for a copy of your child's IEP, your school must give you one free. In some states, schools must provide a copy of the IEP even if you do not ask for it.

More information about your right to a free copy of the IEP is at 34 C.F.R. §300.324(a)(6), 300.322(f), and in the Commentary, FR, Vol. 71, No. 156, 46679, 46687 (2006).

Your school must give you progress reports on your child at least as often as parents of nondisabled children receive report cards.

More information about progress reports is at 34 C.F.R. §300.320(a)(3)(ii) and in the *Commentary*, FR, Vol. 71, No. 156, 46664 (2006).

Right Number Two: To Give Information about Your Child

You are a goldmine of information and know your child better than anyone else. After all, you were your child's first teacher.

You may be the only member of the school team who knows your child in the world outside of school. You see your child in many more environments, at home, in the community, in the neighborhood, and in real-life situations.

You know how your child interacts with strangers, neighbors, friends, and family.

Most school days are about six hours long. This is a small snapshot of time during the day.

You are around your child almost three times longer than most people at school. You have more information and experience about your child than anyone else. You are the expert in the room!

Your school cannot offer your child a FAPE unless it has the valuable information only available from you! That information should always be a part of the IEP.

When your school evaluates or reevaluates your child, you must have a chance to express concerns and make recommendations and suggestions about what your child needs. Your school must include this as part of its data collection.

You have a right to provide information about your child in a written report. Some parents give a Parent Report to the IEP team. You will learn more about this in Lesson Seven.

More information about parent participation is at 34 C.F.R. §§300.304, §300.322, §300.327, §300.328, and 300.501(b) and (c). A right to voice concerns is at 34 C.F.R. 300.324(a)(ii) and (b)(1)(ii)(C). A right to give the school a written report in the *Commentary*, FR, Vol. 71, No. 156, 46678 and 46688 (2006).

Right Number Three: A Right to Disagree.

You don't have to agree to everything your school wants to do about your child's education. You can disagree at any time by filing a state complaint, a due process complaint, or asking for mediation.

You will learn more about complaints later in this lesson and due process complaints in Lesson Eleven.

More information about the parents' right to disagree is at 34 C.F.R. §§300.502 (b), 300.506, 300.532, 300.140 and in the *Commentary*, FR, Vol. 71, No. 156, 46678 (2006).

State Complaints

Anyone can file a state complaint, even they live out of state. These types of complaints are filed with the state DOE when someone thinks a school is not following the IDEA or a state's special education law. You can ask another person to help you file a state complaint.

A state complaint must be in writing. It must include certain things. Your NOPS will tell what must be in a complaint, or you can contact your state DOE for more information.

Each state must have a model state complaint form. Sometimes these model forms are on the DOE website. If you can't find one there, call your DOE and ask it to send you the form.

You don't have to use the state's model form. However, if you use it, your complaint is more likely to include everything your state requires.

You must send a copy of your complaint to your school _and_ to your state DOE. You will receive a decision from your DOE within 60 calendar days. You must file a state complaint within one year from the time you learn about a violation.

Send all proof of your allegations along with your complaint. Never assume the DOE will have access to everything. You can continue to send evidence as long as the investigation is not complete.

You can learn more about state complaints by looking at investigation reports. Sometimes these are posted on the DOE website. Studying these reports may help you write a better complaint.

A state complaint is different from a due process complaint. State complaints usually involve systemic violations of law that affect more than one child. A due process complaint is about a disagreement between a parent and a school about one specific child.

Due Process complaints can be about identification, eligibility, educational evaluations, special education services, placement, or any other dispute about whether a child is receiving a FAPE.

If you file a state complaint and a due process complaint, your DOE will not investigate the state complaint until your hearing is over. This is true even if you file the state complaint before you file a Due Process Complaint.

More information about state and due process complaints is at 34 C.F.R. §§300.140, 300.151, 300.152, 300.153, 300.504(c)(5), and model complaint forms at §300.509 and in the Commentary, FR, Vol. 71, No. 156, 46693 (2006).

Civil Rights Complaints

The Office for Civil Rights (OCR) investigates complaints based on disability discrimination. Filing an OCR complaint is similar to filing a state complaint but with different deadlines.

You must file an OCR complaint within 180 calendar days from the date of the last discriminatory action.

Under certain conditions, you can ask the OCR to "toll" the deadline. If OCR agrees to do this, it will put aside the 180-day filing requirement.

One example of tolling the deadline is if a violation is ongoing and goes beyond the 180-day deadline.

You can file an OCR complaint on discrimination that affects one child or a group of children. When the OCR investigates the complaint, it will compare the treatment of the child or children to the treatment of *nondisabled children.*

The OCR website publishes complaint investigation reports under the topic "Reading Room." A link is included in the Appendix.

Reading these reports will help you understand how OCR investigates complaints. It may also help you write a better complaint.

Another helpful resource is the Case Processing Manual. It gives details about the procedure OCR uses to investigate complaints. A link to the Manual is in the Appendix.

Filing an OCR complaint with the wrong regional office or the Washington D.C. office may delay the investigation. The Appendix includes a list of OCR's Regional Offices.

FERPA Complaints

If you believe your school violated FERPA, you can file a complaint with the Student Privacy Policy Office (SPPO). Children who are at least 18 years old can file complaints on their own.

You must file a FERPA complaint within 180 days from the time you learned about the violation. If the offense is ongoing, you can ask to toll the deadline.

A FERPA complaint must be in writing and must include any facts that prove the violation. Send any proof you have along with the complaint.

You can file a FERPA complaint online or mail it to:

U.S. Department of Education
Student Privacy Policy Office
400 Maryland Ave, SW
Washington, DC 20202-8520

More information about FERPA complaints is at 34 C.F.R. §§99.63 – 99.67.

Right Number Four: Due Process.

The right to due process is one of your most important rights. You and your child have separate due process rights. You will learn more about Due Process and Alternative Dispute Resolution in Lesson Eleven.

It Really is This Simple.

As you continue to learn about special education, you will learn about other rights and safeguards. Most of them will easily fit under one or more of the four rights listed in this lesson.

Since this book aims to make special education as simple as possible, for now, just remember your four basic rights.

Transfer of Parent's Rights

The age a child becomes an adult is decided by state law. In most states, this is age 18. According to state law, when a child becomes an adult, the parents' rights transfer to the child. The exception to this is if your child is legally incompetent.

After the transfer of rights, the child decides whether the parent continues to be involved in educational decisions.

You must help your child learn to be a self-advocate. The IEP must include measurable self-advocacy goals as early as possible.

More information about the transfer of rights is at 34 C.F.R. §300.520 and in the Commentary, FR, Vol. 71, No. 156, 46545, 46668, 46671, 46713, and 46737 (2006).

If you remember only one thing from this lesson, please remember your four rights: (1) to be an equal team member, (2) to give the school information about your child, (3) to disagree; and (4) to due process.

Lesson Summary

In this lesson, you learned about rights and safeguards, complaints, and the transfer of your rights to your adult child. Next you will learn about Child Find, Referrals, and Response to Intervention.

LESSON FOUR: Child Find, Referrals and RtI

Children are like wet cement. Whatever falls on them makes an impression. – Haim Ginott

Child Find

How does your child get into special education? You learned in Lesson One that you shouldn't have to do anything at all because of IDEA's Child Find provision.

As part of Child Find, schools must find, evaluate, and identify all children with disabilities who live within their district. This includes those who are highly mobile, migrants, or who attend private and religious schools.

Sadly, all too often, you must help the school "find" your child.

If you do not know how to refer your child, he or she may get lost in the system. That will delay special education services and harm your child. Children with disabilities must have specialized instruction as early as possible!

Do not feel guilty if you hear statements like, "You should have told us your child needs special education!" "Have you asked your child's doctor whether medicine will help?" We cannot help your child until you get the behaviors under control!"

Your school should not make your child feel guilty with inappropriate statements like, "You need to try harder." "You are lazy and unmotivated." "You have to learn to control your behavior."

A disability is not your or your child's fault! Your school must "find" all children with disabilities.

The school is on the front lines. School staff should be the first to notice when a child struggles or fails to make progress. After all, they are the education experts.

Schools are responsible for seeing and addressing early signs of learning problems. Ignoring or taking a "wait and see" approach doesn't fulfill the Child Find mandate.

You should also not accept statements like, "Yes. Your child is struggling, but others in the class are much worse off!" The issue is not about other children; it is *about your child!*

How would you feel if you took your child to the doctor only to hear, "Yes, your child has cancer. But I have other patients with cancer who are much worse off." Don't let anyone dismiss your concerns about your child this easily!

More about Child Find is at 34 C.F.R. §§300.111 and 300.131, and in the Commentary, FR, Vol. 71, No. 156, 46541 – 46542, 46546, 46584, 46589 – 46593, 46597, 46600, 46632, 46636 – 46637, 46647, 46727, 46730, 46736 (2006).

The first step you can take to help your school "find" your child is to understand the referral process. This section will teach you how to "refer" your child for an "initial evaluation."

Asking for an Initial Evaluation

Before a child can receive special education services, someone must make a referral for an initial evaluation. "Referral" is not the same as "Child Find."

Anyone can make a Child Find referral. But, unless your state law says differently, only a parent or a public agency can make a referral for an initial evaluation.

A "public agency" does not include an employee, such as a teacher or related services provider, unless they act for the public agency.

An initial evaluation referral must be in writing. Adding your consent to the referral means the 60-day evaluation deadline begins when a school official receives it.

The IDEA does not require a parent to use a specific form to give consent for an evaluation.

A referral can be a letter, an email, or a text message, as long as it includes the date and your signature. Keep a copy of the referral for your own records.

More referral information is at 34 C.F.R. §300.301(b) and in the *Commentary*, FR, Vol. 71, No. 156, 46636 (2006).

Your school must tell you in writing whether it will or will not evaluate your child. If it refuses, the written notice must say so. If it agrees to evaluate, the notice must say what kind of testing it will do.

More information about the notice requirements is at 34 C.F.R. §§300.304 and 300.503(b) and in the *Commentary* at FR, Vol 71, No. 156, 46636 (2006).

What if the school wants to test your child and you disagree? You do not have to agree to the testing. If you refuse to give consent, your school can ask for a hearing.

Suppose the Independent Hearing Officer (IHO) or Administrative Law Judge (ALJ) orders an evaluation. In that case, your school can test without your consent. You can appeal that decision. You will learn more about hearings and appeals in Lesson Eleven.

Before you say no to testing, you may want to meet with your school to see why it thinks an evaluation is needed. That will give you a chance to get any of your questions answered about the testing.

You will learn more about Evaluations and Reevaluations, including the Initial Evaluation in Lesson Five.

The Evaluation Report

The school must give you a free copy of the evaluation report. If there is a deadline for giving you the evaluation report, it will be in your state law and the NOPS.

Evaluation reports should be clearly written so everyone can understand the testing results. The report must explain how your child learns and what type of instruction should work the best.

The report should explain your child's strengths, weaknesses, abilities, and achievements. It should describe how the disability affects educational performance. It should list all your child's needs, *even those not linked to the disability or disability category!*

Teachers should be able to look at an evaluation report and understand how to teach the child. The report should tell the IEP team what a child needs in the way of special education, related services, supports, and accommodations.

The report should say whether your child appears to have a disability and needs special education and related services. However, the IEP team is responsible for making the final eligibility decision.

If your child is eligible, the evaluation report must include enough information to help the team write an IEP.

If you disagree with the evaluation, you can ask for an Independent Educational Evaluation (IEE) at the school's cost. You will learn more about IEEs in Lesson Five.

More information about evaluation reports is at 34 C.F.R. §§300.301(c)(2), 300.306(a)(1), 300.321 and in the *Commentary*, FR, Vol. 71, No. 156, 46643, 46645, 46660, 46678 (2006).

The Eligibility Meeting

When the testing is finished, your school will invite you to an eligibility meeting. Someone must be there who can explain the testing results, the instructional implications and answer your questions.

You and the other team members will discuss the evaluation data and additional available information.

After a full discussion of the evaluation results and other data, the team will decide whether your child is eligible for special education. If eligibility is determined, the team chooses the eligibility category.

Remember that the program, services, and placement are based on your child's needs, not on the disability category the team chooses.

The purposes of disability categories are to count the number of children with each type of disability and to provide your school with special education funding.

You can ask for a due process hearing if you don't agree with the eligibility decision. You will learn more about eligibility and disability categories in Lesson Six and due process hearings in Lesson Eleven.

More information about evaluations is at 34 C.F.R. §§300.305, eligibility at §300.306 and in the *Commentary* at FR, Vol. 71, No. 156 46543 – 46545, 46549, 46636 (2006), and disability categories at 34 C.F.R. §§300.8 and in the *Commentary*, FR, Vol. 71, No. 156, 46548 – 46551, 46582, 46655, 46659 – 46660 (2006).

The team must write an IEP as soon as possible after finding a child eligible. Some schools do this immediately after the eligibility meeting. Others meet later to write the IEP.

In any case, an IEP must be completed within 30 days from the day the team finds a child eligible. Services in the IEP must be available as soon as possible after the IEP is completed.

The IEP must address all your child's needs, even if they are not linked to the disability or the disability category.

You will learn more about the IEP and the IEP team in Lesson Seven.

More information about the IEP is at 34 C.F.R. §§300.320, 300.323(c), and in the *Commentary*, FR, Vol. 71, No. 156, 46661, 46680 (2006).

Response to Intervention

In 2004, Congress added Response to Intervention (RtI) to the IDEA to screen children suspected of having a Specific Learning Disability (SLD).

Congress believed children's academic achievement and behavior would improve if SLDs were identified early. Another purpose of RtI was to keep children from needlessly being placed in special education.

Schools *may* use RtI as part of the evaluation process. IDEA strongly suggests but does not require schools to use RtI.

Suppose a child's academic achievement improves when provided with RtI scientific, research-based interventions. If so, they may not need special education.

RtI is voluntary; you do not have to agree to have your child participate. RtI can be provided at the same time your school is evaluating your child. If RtI data is tracked accurately, it can add valuable information to the evaluation process.

Suppose a child fails to make progress in a RtI program. In that case, schools must immediately ask permission to do an initial evaluation. *This does not always happen!*

Some children linger in RtI programs for years before anyone asks for an evaluation. All too often, schools leave it up to the parents to refer the child.

Some schools place children with all types of disabilities in RtI programs. This was not the intent of Congress. RtI was added *only* for children suspected of having specific learning disabilities.

Your school may say your child must participate in RtI program before it can make an evaluation referral. That is not true.

Schools cannot use RtI to delay or deny an evaluation. In fact,

Congress said schools can use RtI as *part* of the evaluation process.

Before you say no to RtI services, you may want to consider how long it takes to initiate special education. The deadline for initial evaluations is 60 school days. Your state may have a different timeline. That's a long time for any child to wait for services!

In the meantime, RtI services may give your child some help. Be sure to tell your school you are not waiving the evaluation deadlines while your child is in RtI.

More information about RtI is at 34 C.F.R. §§300.307(a)(2), 300.309(a)(2)(i), 300.309(c)(1), and 300.311(a)(7) and in the *Commentary*, FR Vol. 71, No. 156, 46543, 46646 - 46647, 46648 (2006)

Ban on Forced Medication

Some schools tell parents their child must take medication before they will provide special education. Some even tell parents they will not evaluate until a child is on medication.

This is simply not true. The IDEA banned forced medication in 2004!

Whether your child takes medication is a decision made by your child's doctor and you. Your school cannot deny evaluations or special education services because you don't want to give your child medications.

More information about the ban on forced medication is at 34 C.F.R. §300.174 and in the *Commentary*, FR Vol. 71, No. 156, 46622, (2006).

If you remember only one thing from this lesson, please remember this: Your school is responsible for "finding" your child. You may have to make a written initial evaluation referral.

Lesson Summary

In this lesson, you learned about Child Find, referral, initial evaluations, RtI, and the ban against forced medication. Next you will learn about evaluations, reevaluations, private evaluations, and IEEs.

LESSON FIVE: Evaluations and Reevaluations

"The potential possibilities of any child are the most intriguing and stimulating in all creation." — Ray L. Wilbur, third president of Stanford University

Learning About Tests

To be the best advocate for your child, you must become an expert in tests and scores. Some parents think they need a college education to understand tests and scores.

Don't count yourself out. Understanding tests is not rocket science.

Many parents just like you have become experts in understanding what tests and scores mean. Some know more about them than the average teacher! With a bit of study, you can become an expert in tests and scores.

You can learn what tests are supposed to measure and use test scores to write a better IEP.

The Appendix includes several resources to help you learn more about tests and evaluations.

The Initial Evaluation

When your school agrees to evaluate your child for the first time, it must do a comprehensive, full, and individual evaluation (FIE).

This means tests must be given one-on-one. Schools must assess children in all areas of the suspected disability.

Unless your state has a different deadline, an initial evaluation must be completed within 60 days from the time you give your written consent.

Your state's deadline should be in your NOPS. If you can't find it there, call your state DOE.

When testing a child, schools must use several tools and strategies and more than one test. Your state law may have information about the minimum tests a school must use.

An evaluator can test in more areas, but not less than the state's basic requirements.

Using several different tests gives the evaluator more accurate results. It also offers better information to the IEP team to decide eligibility and write an IEP.

Tests are available to measure sensory processing, adaptive behavior, post-school skills, executive functioning, and auditory processing.

Some states require a Functional Behavioral Assessment (FBA) for some disability categories. You will learn more about FBAs in Lesson Ten.

An evaluator must use technically sound, impartial, unbiased, valid, reliable, and fair tests.

A valid test measures what it is supposed to measure. A reliable test gives similar results each time it is performed. A fair test is not biased against any particular group, race, or culture.

The evaluator must test your child in the same language and mode of communication used in the home and be fluent in that language. Interpreters should be used only as a last resort.

Tests must measure what children can do, not what they can't do. Special tests are available to use with children who are blind, deaf, have speech, language, sensory, fine motor problems, or cognitive weaknesses.

Specialized tests should be used if a child's disability might get in the way of or influence the testing.

Evaluators also have different ways to administer tests to accommodate children who have specific disabilities. Tests must be chosen with care to ensure fair and valid estimates of a child's abilities and achievement.

An evaluator may need to use a "non-standard administration" of a test. If so, the report must explain why this was done and what effect it had on the results.

Evaluations must compare your child's knowledge and skills to other children of the same age. This includes functional skills your child will need for success in school and in the real world outside.

The initial evaluation may find your child has more than one disability. For example, your child can have both a specific learning disability and attention deficit disorder.

Even a single disability can have an adverse effect on several academic and functional areas. Problems with reading, writing, spelling, or learning arithmetic will challenge your child in every school subject that uses those skills.

If test or subtest scores show a weakness, these areas should be targeted with specific tests. Looking into those areas may help explain why a child is failing to progress.

In general, the more evaluation information the IEP team has, the better the IEP will be.

More information about initial evaluations is at 34 C.F.R. §§300.301 and determination of eligibility is at 300.306 and in the *Commentary*, FR, Vol. 71, No. 156, 46543, 46567, 46584, 46592, 46630 – 46632, 46635, 46637, 46643, 46750 (2006).

Ability (IQ) Testing

Some people may warn against testing a child's IQ. They may say if IQ scores are below average, teachers may lower their expectations.

In 2017, the U.S. Supreme Court ruled that all special education children have a right to an "appropriately ambitious" educational program and must be given a chance to meet "challenging objectives."

The *Endrew F.* case confirms the Supreme Court's desire to improve academic outcomes for all children with disabilities. You should no longer fear an IQ score will allow your school to lower the bar for your child. *Endrew F. v. Douglas County School District*, Re-1, 137 S. Ct. 988.

IQ testing can be helpful. It can explain why a child learns better one way than another. This helps teachers know how what instruction works best.

Some states do not require IQ testing at all. Others make evaluators use it only for specific disabilities. If your state does not require ability testing, you can still ask the school to do it.

Schools commonly use the Wechsler Intelligence Scale for Children, 5th Edition (WISC-V). Other IQ tests include the Differential Ability Scales, 2nd Edition (DAS-II), and the Woodcock-Johnson Tests of

Cognitive Abilities, 3rd Edition (W-J III COG). All these IQ tests rely to a certain extent on verbal abilities.

Suppose a child has verbal weaknesses, speech or language problems, or Dyslexia. In that case, the evaluator may want to consider using a nonverbal IQ test. An IQ test that relies on verbal abilities *in any way* may not give accurate results of what your child can do.

Some children appear to score low on IQ tests even when their ability level is actually higher. This happens if the wrong IQ test is used, causing the child's ability scores to be "artificially depressed" by the disability.

If you suspect this, you can ask the evaluator to confirm the results from the first test with a different type of IQ test. An inaccurate IQ score is not helpful information.

An evaluator who thinks an IQ score is inaccurate must say so and explain why they believe this.

Comparing IQ and achievement scores can help determine whether a child has a specific learning disability. In general, achievement scores should come close to matching a child's ability scores.

When achievement scores are considerably lower than the IQ scores, a child could have a learning disability.

When achievement scores are higher than the IQ scores, it also might mean expectations were set too low for the child. If expectations are set too low, your child may not have had a chance to meet "challenging objectives."

Achievement scores higher than ability scores can also mean the IQ test did not accurately measure the child's ability level.

Testing results may show "scatter." Scatter is when there

are large differences between the subtest scores.

Subtest scores usually cluster within a few points of each other. When you look at the evaluation report, the pattern of scores should not be spread out widely.

Compare the scores in the left column of Table 2 with the scores in the right column to see what scatter looks like. In the first column, the scores cluster close together.

Notice the wide gaps between the scores in the second column. That is what "scatter" looks like. Scatter can occur on IQ testing or on achievement testing.

Scatter can mean several different things and is a discussion beyond the scope of this lesson. When you notice unusual differences in subtest scores, ask the examiner to explain the reason for the scatter.

Woodcock–Johnson IV Tests of Achievement Subtest Scores Average Range – 90–110		
Typical Pattern		Pattern Showing Scatter
Letter Word ID	96	90
Passage Comp.	95	72
Word Attack	100	70
Oral Reading	102	75
Sentence Reading Fluency	97	80
Applied Problem	98	102
Calculation	103	117
Math Facts Fluency	100	114
Spelling	97	77
Writing Samples	109	89
Sentence Writing Fluency	102	79
Table 2		

Achievement Testing

School evaluations must include achievement tests. The IEP team uses this information to see whether your child is eligible for special education. Information from reevaluations helps to see if a child is making academic progress.

Achievement tests measure a child's general knowledge in specific subjects or skill areas. These tests usually assess reading, writing, spelling, written language, and mathematics. Some tests also measure achievement in social studies, science, and humanities.

Commonly used achievement tests include the Wechsler Individual Achievement Test (WIAT), the Woodcock-Johnson IV Tests of Achievement (WJ-IV), and the Kaufman Test of Educational Achievement (KTEA-3).

No one achievement test is designed to measure every part of an academic area. Comprehensive evaluations include specific tests that target specific subject areas.

For example, a comprehensive reading assessment would include, *at a minimum,* vocabulary, reading comprehension, reading fluency, phonics, and phonemic awareness testing.

A comprehensive mathematics evaluation would include calculation, number sense, problem-solving, reasoning, and any other needed area.

Since no one test measures all these areas, an evaluator may want to administer additional specific tests.

A complete evaluation should tell an IEP team what type of problems a child has and why he or she has them. This includes academic and functional areas.

Remember that reading, writing, and vocabulary problems affect most academics since they all rely on good reading, writing, and communication skills.

Evaluations can show scores in several different ways. You may see results reported with Standard Scores (SS), Scaled Scores (ss), T Scores (TS), Percentile Ranks (PR), Age Equivalents (AE or chronological), and/or Grade Equivalents (GE).

Standard Scores are the most reliable measures of achievement. However, most people find it easier to understand percentile ranks. It is easy to misunderstand age and grade level scores and vague terms like "below average," "average," and "above average."

School evaluations must include achievement tests. The IEP team uses achievement test scores to see whether a child is eligible for special education. In reevaluations, the information tells the team whether the child is making academic progress.

Be careful when looking at test results that use vague terms. "Average" may not mean what you think it means. Look at the Bell Curve in Figure 1. Can you see that "average" (85-115) is an extremely broad range of scores?

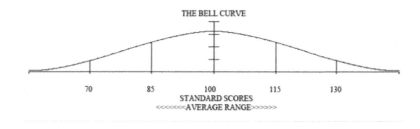

Figure 1

Many schools use group achievement tests to assess all children. Some commonly used group tests are the **NWEA**, the California Achievement Test, and the Iowa Test of Basic Skills. These tests may show scores as **GE** or **AE** instead of in **SS**.

Group achievement test scores can provide extra information about how a child performs. The **IEP** team should never use them solely to make eligibility or placement decisions since they are not individually administered.

The most reliable tests are those given one-on-one to your child. That's why the **IDEA** says your school must do a Full *Individual* Evaluation (**FIE**).

More information about testing, evaluations, and evaluation procedures is at 34 **C.F.R.** §§300.301, 300.302, 300.303, 300.304, 300.305, 300.309 and in the *Commentary*, **FR**, Vol. 71, No. 156, 46642 – 46644, 46651, 46654, 46743, 46746 (2006).

Reevaluations

Children in special education must be reevaluated regularly to measure progress and see whether they are still eligible for special education. A reevaluation must include input and information from the parents.

Suppose the results of an outside private or independent evaluation are available. In that case, the **IEP** team must consider those results during the meeting.

If a child is struggling, not making progress, or has other academic, functional, or behavior problems, he or she can be reevaluated before the three years are up.

A child must be reevaluated at least every three years or more often if needed unless you and your school agree that there is no need for one.

What should you do if your school says it has enough information and does not want to reevaluate your child? Before you agree to not do a reevaluation, think carefully. Ask yourself these questions.

How long has it been since your child's last reevaluation? Was it more than a year ago? The IEP team needs "current" information for the Present Levels of Academic Achievement and Functional Performance section of the IEP.

You will learn more about the Present Levels in Lesson Seven.

Is your child still struggling? If so, a reevaluation should be done to tell you why the problems are not going away.

Reevaluations may suggest more or different services and support for your child.

You know it is wise to take your child to the doctor for regular medical checkups. Regular examinations help your child stay healthy. Do you wait three years to take your child for a medical checkup?

You may want to think of reevaluations as "educational checkups" that help keep your child's education healthy.

Unless you and your school agree otherwise, reevaluations can be limited to one per year. You must give your written consent for each reevaluation.

Your school must reevaluate children before removing or "exiting" them from special education unless they have earned a regular diploma or have "aged out" of special education.

Each state decides at what age a child ages out of special education. Some states provide services beyond the IDEA maximum age of 21.

Other types of Evaluations and Reevaluations

Evaluations and reevaluations are not just about school subjects and your child's IQ. Your child must be assessed in every area of the suspected disability.

This means an FIE may need to assess a child's gross and fine motor skills, sensory processing, auditory processing, and speech/language skills.

At a minimum, the following areas should be assessed. This is not a complete list.

☞ Current Information about your Child.
☞ Teacher and Staff Observations.
☞ Social/Emotional status.
☞ Academic Achievement and Performance.
☞ Current classroom information.
☞ Health, Vision, Hearing.
☞ General Intelligence/Ability.
☞ Behavior, including Adaptive Behavior.
☞ Motor Skills.
☞ Speech/Language Development.
☞ Functional Performance.
☞ Developmental status.
☞ Ability to take part in PE.
☞ Social Skills.

More information about reevaluations is at 34 C.F.R. §§300.303(b)(2), 300.304(c)(3), 300.305(a)(2)(B), 300.321(a)(5), 300.305(e) and in the *Commentary*, FR, Vol. 71, No. 156, 46593, 46630, 46635, 46640 – 46643, 46648, 46688 46746, (2006).

Independent Evaluations

Parents can be good judges of their child's strengths and weaknesses. Suppose you believe your school's evaluation is not accurate or comprehensive. In that case, you can disagree with it and ask for an Independent Educational Evaluation (IEE) at school cost.

Your school may ask why you disagree. You do not have to give an answer. Your request for an **IEE** cannot be denied just because you will not tell the school why you disagree with its evaluation.

You can ask for one **IEE** for each school evaluation or reevaluation with which you disagree. Your school must pay for the **IEE**, or it must ask for a hearing to prove its assessment was appropriate.

The cost of an **IEE** must be reasonable. Schools may create criteria that explain what it considers to be a "reasonable" cost.

If your child needs an **IEE** that is more costly than the allowed criteria, the school must give you a chance to explain why the cost criteria should not apply.

Your school can also set criteria for independent evaluators. Be sure to get a copy of your school's **IEE** policy before you choose an evaluator. Your school may not have to pay for the **IEE** if the person you choose does not meet its criteria.

Upon request, your school must give you a list of **IEE** evaluators that meet its criteria. *You don't have to choose someone from that list.* You can select any evaluator who meets the school's criteria.

The person you choose should have no relationship or connection to your school. You can use a neuropsychologist, a psychologist, or a school psychologist.

More information about **IEE**s is at 34 **C.F.R.** §300.502, and in the *Commentary*, **FR**, **Vol.** 71, **No.** 156, 46690 (2006), and **OSEP**, *Letter to Parker*, 2004.

Private Evaluations

At any time, you can choose to pay for a private evaluation. The evaluations and evaluators must also meet your school's **IEE** criteria.

You don't have to share the private evaluation results with your school. If you don't share the results, the evaluation is not considered an **IEE**.

If you share the results of a private evaluation, the **IEP** team must consider them. "Consider" does not mean the team must accept the results.

More information about private evaluations is at 34 **C.F.R.** 300.502(c) and in the *Commentary*, FR Vol. 71, **No.** 156, 46690 (2006).

Evaluations and the Present Levels

The team uses the evaluation results, your input, and any other available information to develop the **IEP**'s Present Levels of Academic Achievement and Functional Performance. You will learn more about the Present Levels and the **IEP** in Lesson Seven.

If you remember only one thing from this lesson, please remember this: It is just as important for you to understand tests and scores as it is for you to know about the law.

Lesson Summary

In this lesson, you learned about initial evaluations, reevaluations, independent and private evaluations, as well as their deadlines. Next you will learn about eligibility and disability.

LESSON SIX: Eligibility and Disability

> *Disability is a natural part of the human experience and in no way diminishes the right of individuals to participate in or contribute to society. 20 U.S.C. §1400(c)*

What is a Child with a Disability?

A child can have a disability, condition, or diagnosis and not be eligible for special education.

To be a "child with a disability," two things must be true: (1) the child must have a disability that has an adverse effect on educational performance; and (2) as a result of the disability, the child must need special education and related services.

In some states, a child who needs only related services and not special instruction will not be eligible for special education. In other states, children can qualify even if they need only related services. Your state's **DOE** or your state's special education law can tell you which is true where you live.

A child does not have to fail, make failing grades, or be held back to qualify for special education. Children can be eligible even if they make good grades and are being promoted from grade to grade.

More information about disabilities and eligibility is at 34 **C.F.R.** §§300.8(a)(2), 300.101(c) and in the

Commentary, FR, Vol. 71, No. 156, 46549, 46580 (2006).

IDEA Disabilities

The IDEA includes a list of disability categories and their definitions. These may help you understand whether your child might be eligible for special education. Your state law may have more details about disability categories.

Autism

Autism is a developmental disability. It can significantly affect a child's verbal and nonverbal communication and social interaction. If autism adversely affects educational performance, the child will usually qualify.

Autism is generally noticed before a child is three years old. They may have repetitive behavior, stereotyped movements, unusual sensory responses. They may resist changes in routines.

Deaf-Blindness

Children who are deaf and blind have disabilities that are more severe than if they were just deaf or blind. Often these children have severe communication problems. Helen Keller is an excellent example of a child with deaf-blindness. A deaf-blind child has more significant needs than a child who is deaf or who is blind.

Deafness

A hearing impairment severe enough to affect a child's ability to process spoken information usually has an adverse effect on educational performance. It can be a qualifying disability even if the child uses a hearing aid or a cochlear implant.

Emotional Disturbance

An emotional disturbance must have gone on for an extended time and have an adverse effect on a child's education. It must not be caused by an intellectual disability or a sensory or health issue.

Characteristics of an emotional disability include an inability to make or keep satisfactory social and personal relationships with peers and teachers, inappropriate behavior or feelings in normal situations, a general and constant feeling of unhappiness or depression, or physical symptoms or fears associated with personal or school problems.

Hearing Impairment

A consistent and lasting or fluctuating hearing loss that has an adverse effect on educational performance can be a qualifying disability. It is a different category than deafness.

Intellectual Impairment

A child with an intellectual impairment has a significantly below-average IQ with deficits in adaptive behavior. When the impairment has an adverse effect on educational performance, it can be a qualifying disability.

Generally, intellectual disabilities are noted during the developmental period.

Multiple Disabilities

Sometimes children have more than one disability that causes severe problems. They cannot be educated in a program designed for children with single disabilities. If multiple disabilities have an adverse effect on educational performance, these children may qualify under this category.

Children who are deaf and blind will not usually qualify here. They could be eligible under the deaf-blind category.

Orthopedic Impairment

A severe orthopedic impairment that has an adverse effect on educational performance can be a qualifying disability. Examples of orthopedic impairments include but are not limited to birth defects, disease, cerebral palsy, amputations, and fractures or burns that cause contractures.

Other Health Impairment

Children with chronic or acute disabilities that cause limited strength, vitality, or alertness and adversely affects educational performance may qualify under the Other Health Impairment category.

Examples include, but are not limited to, asthma, diabetes, epilepsy, a heart condition, hemophilia, lead poisoning, leukemia, nephritis, rheumatic fever, sickle cell anemia, and Tourette syndrome.

Children with attention deficit disorder or attention deficit hyperactivity disorder may qualify if the conditions have an adverse effect on educational performance. Sights and sounds in the classroom may distract these children so severely they cannot focus on instruction.

Specific Learning Disability

A Specific Learning Disability (SLD) means the brain can't process information well. A child can have a specific learning disability and have other disabilities. It is also possible for a child to have more than one specific learning disability.

A child may qualify if the learning disability has an adverse effect on educational performance.

An **SLD** can affect a child's ability to understand or use spoken or written language or cause problems with listening, thinking, speaking, reading, writing, spelling, or being able to do arithmetic.

A child with an **SLD** is just as intelligent as any other child. This disability is not an intellectual impairment. In fact, many children with **SLD**s have high, above average, or even superior IQs.

If your school says your child's IQ is too high to qualify under this category, do not believe it. The key is not the IQ but whether the **SLD** has an adverse impact on educational performance.

Early identifying children with **SLD**s and providing specialized instruction often remediates the disability entirely. Unfortunately, this does not always happen.

Too many children with **SLD**s remain in special education for their entire public-school career. They were either identified too late or were not provided with the type of instruction to remediate the **SLD**.

Receiving appropriate specialized instruction in the first and second grades can effectively close the achievement gap between children with **SLD**s and their typical peers.

Many different terms are used to describe specific learning disabilities. You may hear them called perceptual disabilities, brain injury, minimal brain dysfunction, Dyslexia, and developmental aphasia.

Public Law 94-142 defined Dyslexia as a specific learning disability in 1975. Yet more than forty years later, schools largely ignored the term, refusing to acknowledge Dyslexia as a specific learning disability.

Thanks to the massive grassroots efforts of Decoding Dyslexia, schools now must recognize children with Dyslexia and provide early services.

Several things may exclude children from being found eligible under the SLD category.

☞ When a problem is caused mainly by vision, hearing, or motor disabilities.
☞ When the child has an intellectual impairment.
☞ When the child has an emotional disturbance.
☞ When the child was never taught or exposed to a subject.
☞ Problems caused by environmental, cultural, or economic reasons.

These children may qualify under a different category. There may also be help available outside of special education.

Contact your state DOE for information on other available services for children who do not qualify under the SLD category because of the above reasons.

Speech or Language Impairment

A Speech or language impairment is a communication disorder that has an adverse effect on your child's educational performance. These impairments include stuttering, articulation problems, or language or voice impairments.

Traumatic Brain Injury (TBI)

A traumatic brain injury is an open or closed head injury caused by an outside physical force. Head injuries from birth trauma or progressive conditions are not

TBIs. The child may qualify under a different disability category.

TBIs can be severe impairments that cause problems in many different areas. They can affect ability levels, language, memory, attention, reasoning, abstract thinking, judgment, problem-solving, sensory, perceptual, and motor abilities.

A TBI can be a child's only disability, or it can be part of another one. Like other disabilities, the TBI must have an adverse effect on educational performance.

Visual Impairment

Children who are completely blind can qualify under this category. They can be eligible even if there is some sight or the vision impairment is corrected if there is an adverse impact on educational performance.

More information about eligibility categories is at 34 **C.F.R.**§§300.8, 300.307, and in the *Commentary*, FR, Vol. 71, **No.** 156, 46548 – 46551, 46645 – 46648 (2006).

Section 504 Disabilities

Under Section 504, the definition of a disability is much broader and quite different than one under the **IDEA.**

Individuals with disabilities have physical or mental impairments which substantially limit one or more major life activities. They can have a record of an impairment or can be regarded as having an impairment.

A physical or mental impairment is a physiological disorder or condition, cosmetic disfigurement, or anatomical loss affecting one or more of the following body systems: neurological; musculoskeletal; special sense organs; respiratory, including speech organs; cardiovascular; reproductive, digestive, genito-urinary; hematic and lymphatic; skin; and endocrine.

It also means any mental or psychological disorder, such as cognitive impairments, organic brain syndrome, emotional or mental illness, and specific learning disabilities.

Major bodily functions include functions of the bowel, bladder, brain, normal cell growth, immune, endocrine, respiratory, reproductive, circulatory, digestive, and neurological systems.

A major life activity means caring for oneself, performing manual tasks, walking, seeing, hearing, speaking, breathing, learning, and working.

Unlike eligibility under the IDEA, a child's impairment need not have an adverse effect on academic performance to qualify as a disability under Section 504.

More information about Section 504 disabilities is at 34 C.F.R. §104.3(j), (i) and §104.3(j)(2)(i) and (ii), and 154 Cong. Rec. S8342, 8346 (daily ed. Sept. 11, 2008) (statement of the Managers to Accompany S. 3406.

If you remember only one thing from this lesson, please remember this: qualifying for special education under the **IDEA** requires two things: (1) a disability that adversely effects educational performance; and, (2) by reason thereof, the child needs special education and related services.

Lesson Summary

In this lesson you learned about the different disability categories and their definitions under the IDEA and Section 504. Next, you will learn about IEPs and the IEP Team.

LESSON SEVEN:

IEPs and the IEP Team

The IEP is "the centerpiece of the statute's education delivery system for disabled children."
Honig v. Doe, 484 U. S. 305, 311 (1988).

The IEP Process

Best practice in writing IEPs is to use a specific process. Following a step-by-step plan is one way to ensure an IEP provides the supports and services to meet a child's unique needs.

The IEP is the blueprint for the child's education. It should be written with the future in mind and must be based on outcomes.

IEPs must give children a chance to continue their education after leaving public school. Further education can mean college, a trade school or enrolling in an adult training program.

Special education aims to prepare children with disabilities to find and keep a job and live as an adult as independently as possible.

We follow plans for almost everything we do. Writing an IEP is no different.

We use a recipe to bake a cake. When changing the oil in a car, we follow a specific routine. Taking shortcuts, omitting steps, or overlooking something in the process means the cake may not rise, or the car's engine may fail.

It is just as dangerous to take shortcuts when writing an IEP. Failing to follow a process can make a difference in whether a child learns to read, write, spell, and do arithmetic!

Present Levels

Each IEP must include Present Levels of Academic Achievement and Functional Performance. This is the most essential section of the IEP.

Writing an IEP is like putting together a jigsaw puzzle. Each team member brings different pieces of the puzzle to the meeting. Only when all the puzzle pieces are on the table can the team write an appropriate IEP.

Your child is unique. So, each puzzle piece is shaped differently from all the others. Every piece has its place and fits somewhere.

The IEP team takes all the puzzle pieces, puts them together, and draws up a plan for the next year that meets the child's needs.

Some people like to put together the outside pieces of a puzzle first. This makes an outline for the rest of the puzzle. The Present Levels are like the outer pieces of your child's IEP.

Just like a house needs a firm foundation, a good IEP will have solid Present Levels. They form the base on which the rest of the IEP stands.

The Present Levels tell your child's story and explain how he or she is doing academically and functionally *today*. That is why *current* evaluation information is so important.

More information about Present Levels is at 34 C.F.R. §§300.305(a)(2)(B)(ii), 300.320(a)(1) and in the *Commentary*, FR, Vol. 71, No. 156, 46662, 46684, (2006).

The Present Levels address more than reading, writing, and arithmetic. They must state a child's "functional skills." Functional skills are any skills that are not related to academics.

Functional Present Levels tell how your child performs outside of the classroom and outside of school. They state how your child does when in nonacademic settings and participating in extracurricular activities.

While all IEPs must include functional Present Levels, not all children will need functional IEP goals.

More information about Functional and Functional Skills is at 34 C.F.R. §§300.303(a)(1), 300.304(b)(1), 300.320(1)(1) and (2)(i), 300.324(a)(iv), 300.600(b)(1) and in the *Commentary*, FR, Vol. 71, No. 156, 46579 (2006).

The parents' role is critical when the team writes the Present Levels. They may be the only team members who know anything about the child outside of school. Parents hold the most critical pieces of the puzzle that makes up the child.

Information from the parents about the child's functional performance must be included in the Present Levels. Parents' Input allows the team to develop an IEP that offers a program to prepare the child for life outside of school.

The staff at your school probably has a good idea of how your child functions in that setting. But a school day is a small part of an entire day. And a classroom is a tiny part of the world in which children with disabilities will live as adults.

Parents see the big picture. They have known the child longer than anyone else. They see the child in different settings, in the real world, and outside of school.

They have more pieces of the puzzle than anyone else on the team. Even more important, they are the only ones who have a vested interest in seeing their child become an independent, self-sufficient adult!

IDEA's purpose is to make sure schools prepare children with disabilities for "further education, employment, and independent living." To do that, the IEP team must use every piece of the puzzle that makes up a child.

Much of that information comes from parents' experience with their child in the real world outside of school.

You can give the IEP team information about your child in several ways. One way is by using a "Parent Report."

A Parent Report includes information from *your point of view* about your child's successes and struggles, and academic and functional needs, both inside and outside of the school setting.

The **U.S.** Department of Education says you can give information to the IEP team by using a Parent Report. "Parents are free to provide input into their child's IEP through a written report if they so choose." *Commentary*, FR, Vol. 71, No. 156, 46678 (2006).

The Appendix has links to Wrightslaw articles about Parent Reports.

More information about the IEP is at 34 **C.F.R.** §§300.320, 300.323 and in the *Commentary*, FR, Vol. 71, No. 156, 46579, 46662, 46663, 46669 (2006).

IEP Team and IEP Meetings

When the IEP team makes the educational decisions, it is expected to act in the child's best interest. To do its job, all necessary team members must be

at IEP meetings. The following
people are all essential IEP team
members:

- The parents.
- A general education teacher if your child will be in general education.
- At least one special education teacher.
- A school staff member who is licensed to teach or supervise your child's special education program.
- Someone who understands and can explain evaluation results.
- Others invited by you or your school.
- Your child when you decide it is appropriate.

The regular education teacher who attends should be the one who will carry out your child's IEP. If your child has more than one regular education teacher, your school can decide which one should attend.

Your school may ask you to excuse an IEP team member from part or all of an IEP meeting. You must give written consent before any team member can be excused. This is true even if that person's area will not be discussed at the meeting.

If you do not consent, the team member must attend the meeting. When team members are excused, they must give the parents their written input before the meeting.

Before agreeing to excuse team members, ask yourself how important it is for them to be at the meeting. Do they have any information necessary to revise your child's IEP? How well do they know your child? Will they be responsible for carrying out any of the IEP's services?

More information about excusing IEP team members is at 34 C.F.R.

§300.321(e) and in the *Commentary*, FR, Vol 71, No. 156, 46673, 46674, 46675 (2006).

You can ask other people to attend IEP meetings either as a team member or as an observer. The people you invite must have some knowledge or expertise about your child.

You can invite school staff to attend an IEP meeting. But your school decides whether they can attend.

Your school must give you written notice about the purpose, time, and place of IEP meetings and who will be there. You must get the notice early enough so you can arrange to attend.

You and the school must agree to the time and place of the IEP meeting. Your school must make a good faith effort to encourage you to attend. It must keep a record of how its efforts to get you to attend. If you refuse to go to the meeting, your school can hold it without you.

If you cannot attend the IEP meeting in person, your school must offer other ways for you to participate. It can arrange for telephone conference calls or use any other electronic means.

If you have a disability or your native language is other than English, your school must provide accommodations or an interpreter.

You have a right to ask questions, voice concerns, and make recommendations to the IEP team.

If your school uses draft IEPs, it must give you a copy before the meeting. It must also tell you that the draft is open to changes.

More information about the IEP team and IEP team meetings is at 34 C.F.R. §§300.17, 300.22, 300.101, 300.108, 300.112, 300.116(b)(2), 300.321, 300.322, 300.323, 300.324 and in the *Commentary*, FR, Vol 71, No. 156,

46634, 46663, 46669, 46670, 46674 – 46679, 46680, 46681 (2006).

Individual Education Program

The team must consider any input, concerns, and recommendations you offer about your child and the IEP. You can give the team information on how you view your child's challenges, strengths, academic, developmental, and functional needs.

After considering your input and all other available information, the team begins to write the IEP.

IEPs must include *at least* the following:

☞ Present Levels – Academic Achievement.
☞ Present Levels – Functional Performance.
☞ Results from the most recent evaluation.
☞ The disability's effect on the child's involvement and progress in general education.
☞ Academic and nonacademic information.
☞ Measurable annual academic goals
☞ Functional goals, if needed
☞ Benchmarks or short-term objectives (for children who take an alternative test).
☞ How the IEP meets the child's unique needs.
☞ How progress will be assessed.
☞ How often the parent will get progress reports.
☞ The special education, related services, and supplementary aids and services the child will receive.
☞ Any program modifications or supports.
☞ Supports for teachers or staff.
☞ Amount of time the child will be in general education.
☞ How the child will participate in extracurricular and nonacademic activities.
☞ An explanation of why the child cannot participate with non-disabled children.
☞ Academic and functional accommodations.
☞ An explanation of why the child will not take state and school tests.
☞ The date services will begin.
☞ The length of the child's services, where and how often they will be provided.

- For a child who will be 16, goals and adult transition services
- One year before the child reaches adulthood, a notice that the parent's rights will transfer to the student.

If this is an initial or first IEP, you must give your written consent before any IEP services can be delivered to your child. Once you have given permission, your child must receive the IEP services as soon as possible.

Every school staff member who will carry out any part of your child's services must have access to the IEP, even if they didn't attend the IEP meeting.

Transfer IEPs Within the Same State or from Another State

If you move from one school to another within the same school district or within another school district in your state, your new school has two choices. It must either adopt the move-in IEP or develop, adopt, and implement a new IEP.

Until the new school develops, adopts, and implements a new IEP, it must provide your child with services comparable to those in the move-in IEP. "Comparable" means similar or equivalent.

Suppose your child has an active IEP and transfers from a state with different eligibility criteria. In that case, the new school may choose to evaluate to see if your child is under the new state's standards.

This evaluation is *not* a reevaluation; it is an initial evaluation and requires your consent. Once the new school receives your permission, it must complete the assessment within 60 days.

The new school must provide comparable services until

eligibility is established and a new IEP is developed and implemented.

If you disagree with the new school's evaluation, you can ask for a due process hearing. Since this is an initial evaluation, stay put does not apply. You will learn more about hearings and "stay put" in Lesson Eleven.

When your child transfers to a new school, it must promptly ask the old school for your child's records. This includes an existing IEP and anything else related to its provision of special education or related services. The old school must provide the records as quickly as possible.

More information about Transfer IEPs, Comparable services, and Transmittal of Records is at 34 C.F.R. §§300.301 and 300.323 and in the *Commentary*, FR Vol 71, No. 156, 46544, 46617, 46629, 46638, 46681, and 46682 (2006).

Placement and Least Restrictive Environment

The IEP team cannot decide placement until after the IEP is complete. Special education and related services must be provided in a child's Least Restrictive Environment.

The placement must be as close as possible to the child's home, preferably in the child's home school.

You will learn more about Placement and Least Restrictive Environment in Lesson Nine.

More information about Placement and Least Restrictive Environment is at 34 C.F.R. §§300.104, 300.115, 300.116, 300.325, 300.327, 300.501, 300.533 and in the *Commentary*, FR Vol. 71, No. 156, 46541, 46556, (2006)

IEP Disagreements

If you do not like all or part of an IEP, you can give your school a written statement saying you disagree with it. You do not have to say why you disagree with the IEP.

Some state laws call this a "written opinion," a "dissenting opinion," or "written statement." If your state law says nothing about disagreeing with an IEP, you can still give a written opinion.

If you remember only one thing from this lesson, please remember the most important parts of the IEP are the Present Levels of Academic Achievement and Functional Performance.

Lesson Summary

In this lesson, you learned about IEP development, including what must be in an IEP, when your child must receive IEP services, who must attend IEP meetings, transfer IEPs, and written opinions. Next you will learn about related services, supplies, and supports.

LESSON EIGHT:

Related and Other Services

> *Reading and writing, arithmetic and grammar do not constitute education, any more than a knife, fork and spoon constitute a dinner.* — *John Lubbock (1834–1913)*

Related Services

Related services are developmental, corrective, and other support services that schools must provide when a child needs them to benefit from special education. They support a child's physical, emotional, or social development needs.

A child may need related services to participate in extracurricular and other nonacademic activities.

Related services are provided to correct a disability, provide extra support for school success, and prepare a child for life as an adult.

A need for related services depends on a child's identified needs, not on a disability label or category.

Schools do not have to provide, maintain, or replace surgically implanted medical devices or devices with external components, such as cochlear implants. They must see that these devices work as they should while the child is in school or when transporting them and from school.

Children who have medically implanted devices may qualify for other types of related services.

Schools must see that children who have medical devices needed for health and safety reasons work correctly. They are responsible for making sure devices a child needs to breathe, get appropriate nutrition, or use for bodily functions work correctly.

Suppose it is impossible to separate a child's emotional needs from educational needs. In that case, related services may include placement in a residential program with therapeutic and habilitation services.

Examples of Related Services include the following. This is not a complete list.

☞ Special transportation.
☞ Speech-language therapy.
☞ Audiology services.
☞ Assistive Technology services and devices.
☞ Interpreting services, transcription services, CART, C-Print, and TypeWell
☞ Psychological services
☞ Physical and occupational therapy.
☞ Recreation, including therapeutic recreation.
☞ School social work services.
☞ School health and nursing services.
☞ Counseling services, including rehabilitation counseling.
☞ Orientation and mobility services.
☞ Early identification and assessment of a disability.
☞ Medical services for a diagnosis or an evaluation.
☞ Tutoring or remediation.
☞ Parent counseling and training.

More information about related services is at 34 C.F.R.§300.34 and in the *Commentary*, FR, Vol. 71, No. 156, 46541, 46548 – 46549, 46569 – 46575, 46581, 46583 (2006).

Supplementary Aids and Services

Supplementary aids and services provide support to children with disabilities who are in regular education classes, nonacademic settings, and other environments. These services allow them to be in the least restrictive environment possible.

The IEPs of children who need supplementary aids and services to be in their least restrictive environment must include these supports.

Schools must include children with disabilities in settings and environments with typical peers unless this cannot be done satisfactorily even with supplementary aids and services. 34 C.F.R. §300.114(a)(2)(ii).

Don't confuse supplementary aids and services with related services. They are entirely different supports.

Supplementary aids and services enable a child to be involved with nondisabled children to the maximum extent appropriate *in all school settings*. 34 C.F.R. §300.42.

On the other hand, related services are developmental, corrective, and other supportive services that allow children with disabilities to benefit from their *special education* program. 34 C.F.R. §300.34.

A child does not have to be in special education to receive supplementary aids and services. These supports are also available to general education students and can include tutoring and remediation. 34 C.F.R. §300.208(a)(1).

More information about supplementary aids and services is at 34 C.F.R. §§300.42, 300.105, 300.107, 300.114(a)(2)(ii), 300.117, 300.208, 300.320(a)(4) and in the *Commentary* at 46541, 46547, 46552, 46569, 46578, 46580 –

46581, 46583, 46585, 46587 –
46589, 46664 – 46665, 46716,
46719, 46724.

Physical Education

Schools that offer PE to nondisabled children must offer PE to children with disabilities.

Children who can't participate in regular PE with the support of supplementary aids and services must be provided with specially designed PE or adapted PE (APE). A school can't simply waive or excuse the child from PE.

Instruction in PE is not just about fun and games. It is meant to help children develop physical and motor fitness and fundamental motor skills and patterns.

PE can include aquatic and dance skills, individual and group games and sports, intramural and lifetime sports, movement education, and motor development.

More information about PE and APE is at 34 C.F.R. §§300.39(b)(2), 300.108 and in the *Commentary*, at FR, Vol. 71, No. 156, 46577, 46583, 46661 – 46662 (2006).

Assistive Technology and Assistive Technology Services

Assistive technology (AT) is a device, an item, a piece of equipment, a system, or a service

AT Services Include:

Evaluations.
Buying, renting, or supplying AT devices.
Managing and matching related services and interventions with AT devices.
Training your child, teachers, employers, and others in the use of AT devices.

that helps a child develop, keep up, or increase functional abilities.

AT can be something you buy off the shelf in a store or something specially designed for a child. AT services include helping a child find, buy, or use an assistive technology device.

If a child needs AT or AT services, the IEP must include them. If a child needs to use a school-provided AT device at home, the IEP must say this, as well.

More information about Assistive Technology is at 34 C.F.R. §§300.5, 300.6, 300.105, 300.172(d) and in the *Commentary*, at FR, Vol. 71, No. 156, 46541, 46547 – 46548, 46555, 46570, 46571, 46579, 46581, 46585, 46621, 46644, 46665, 46684, 46685, 46740 (2006).

Nonacademic and Extracurricular Activities

Schools must include children with disabilities in all school settings and activities to the maximum extent appropriate with the support of supplementary aids and services.

This includes nonacademic settings, extracurricular activities, meals, recess, tutoring, counseling, athletics, transportation, health services, recreation, special groups or clubs, referral to other agencies, and student employment.

The IEP must list all supports and services to ensure a child's success in all settings and environments.

More information about nonacademic and extracurricular services is at 34 C.F.R. §§300.107, 300.117 and in the *Commentary*, at FR, Vol. 71, No. 156, 46541,

46578, 36583, 46585, 46589, 46666, 46670, (2006).

Other Programs and Services

Children with disabilities have a right to participate in all the same educational programs and services as those offered to nondisabled children. These include, but are not limited to, art, music, industrial arts, consumer and homemaking education, and vocational education.

More information about other educational programs and services is at 34 C.F.R. §300.110.

Transition Services and Vocational Education

Before age 16, or younger if appropriate, the IEP must include a transition plan. The Plan must have measurable postsecondary goals and the services a child needs to reach those goals and to prepare him or her for adult life.

Transition Services are a set of planned activities to help a child learn the skills needed for adult living, including further education, employment, and independent living. These services must address both academic and functional skills.

Transition services are based on a results-oriented process and are made on a case-by-case basis according to a child's needs. They can include special instruction, related services, career training, community work or volunteer experiences, and learning daily living skills.

Children in special education must have a chance to participate in vocational education. This program helps students learn the skills needed to do adult work, volunteer, or do a job that doesn't need a college degree.

More information about transition services and vocational education is at 34 C.F.R. §§300.39, 300.43, 300.320(b), 300.321(b), 300.324(c)(1) and in the *Commentary*, FR, Vol. 71, No. 156, 46577, 46578 – 46579, 46580, 46584, 46667, 46668, 46669, 46671. 46672, 46686, 46751 (2006)

If you remember only one thing from this Lesson, please remember this: your child must be educated and involved with nondisabled children in all academic, extra-curricular, and nonacademic settings, and other programs, to the maximum extent appropriate, unless it cannot be done successfully even with Supplementary Aids and

Lesson Summary

In this lesson, you learned about educational, nonacademic, extracurricular programs and services, related services, supplementary aids and services, vocational education, transition services, and assistive technology. Next you will learn about placement, Least Restrictive Environment, and Inclusion.

LESSON NINE: Placement, LRE, and Inclusion

The cart before the horse is neither beautiful nor useful.
– Henry David Thoreau

Placement

If you are like many parents, you may think "Placement" means the location of your child's special education program. This is not true. Placement is not a street address or a location.

It is the program and environment where a child receives the services in the IEP. Placement is not a specific place, classroom, school, or campus.

Placement is not based on a label, disability, or disability category. It is not okay for a school to say your child must go to a particular program because "That's where we send all the children with speech and language problems."

The IEP team makes placement decisions are made on a case-by-case basis. It makes these decisions only after it develops the IEP and decides what a child needs.

A child's placement is based on needs, goals, related services, supplementary aids and services, assistive technology, and the child's participation in nonacademic and extracurricular activities.

The IEP is the key document the team looks at when deciding placement.

Your school must offer your child a "continuum of placement options." That means it must have more than one placement for your child.

A continuum of alternative placements gives a child the best chance to be educated in the least restrictive environment to the maximum extent appropriate.

When the team finishes the IEP, it looks at the different placement options. The placement is based on which program and environment the IEP can be implemented in the least restrictive environment.

Placement includes a variety of options. It can be a general or special education classroom, in the home, in a hospital, an institution, another setting, or a mixture of those settings. Placement is always based on the child's IEP.

Unless the IEP says otherwise, the first placement option the team must consider is a general education environment, in the child's home school, with supplementary aids and services.

Only if the child cannot be satisfactorily educated there with appropriate support can the team consider other placement options.

If placement is not in the home school, it must be as close as possible to the child's home.

More about the Continuum of Placements, Placement, and Least Restrictive Environment is at 34 C.F.R. §§300.114, 300.115, 300.116, 300.117, 300.327 and in the Commentary, FR, Volume 71, No. 156, pp. 46541, 46553, 46556, 46580, 46585, 46586, 46587, 46588, 46656, 46687 46731(2006), and Conf. Rpt. No. 108-779 (2004).

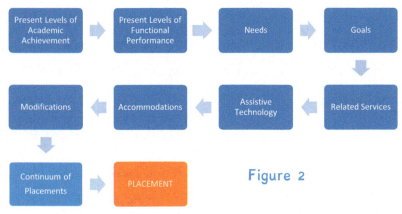

Figure 2 is an example of a process an **IEP** team could follow in developing an **IEP**.

Inclusion and Least Restrictive Environment

You will not find the word "inclusion" in the **IDEA**. The term it uses is Least Restrictive Environment (**LRE**).

LRE means a child will be placed in a general education setting, with nondisabled children, to the maximum extent appropriate, with the support of supplementary aids and services. The **IEP** team decides the child's Least Restrictive Environment.

The team must consider a general education setting as the first placement unless the disability is so severe a child can't be educated there, even with supplementary aids and services.

If necessary, a school can change the curriculum or academic content to support a child's needs. Teachers might need to change the way they present materials or subjects.

A school cannot remove a child from a general education setting solely because the curriculum must be modified.

Regardless of the placement and Least Restrictive Environment, the child must have a chance to meet the same state academic standards that schools expect from nondisabled students.

Below is a list of common supports schools use to successfully place a child in the general education environment. This is not a complete list.

☞ Supplementary aids and services.
☞ Related services.
☞ Assistive technology.
☞ A notetaker or scribe.
☞ Resource room services.
☞ Changing, adapting, or modifying the general education program or curriculum.
☞ Classroom paraprofessionals, instructional assistants, dedicated aides.
☞ Accommodations for the child.
☞ Modifying the classroom environment or the curriculum.

More information about Least Restrictive Environment is at 34 C.F.R. §300.114 through 300.120,

and in the *Commentary*, FR, Vol. 71, No. 156, 46569, 46670, 46585-35486 (2006).

Unilateral Placements

If you believe your school is not providing a **FAPE,** you consider placing your child in a private school. A private school can be an elementary or secondary school and includes religious schools.

If you want the school to pay for the private school, there are specific steps you must follow. If you do not follow these steps, your school may not have to pay for the private placement.

You *must* inform your school *in writing*, (a) you are rejecting its proposed **IEP,** (b) you are *withdrawing* your child, and (c) *enrolling them in a private school.* You must also (d) tell the school *your concerns* and (e) *you want it to pay for the private school.*

You must do all the above either *at the most recent IEP meeting or at least 10 business days before removing your child from the public school.*

The ten days include any holidays that occur on a business day.

You must follow these rules *exactly* to have a chance for reimbursement or payment of the private placement.

Your school will not have to pay for the private placement if it has made a **FAPE** available to your child in a timely manner. It may not have to pay for the private school that placement there is inappropriate.

You may have to file for a due process hearing to get your school to pay for the private placement. An **IHO** or **ALJ** can order your school to pay for it.

If you place your child in a private school, your child is entitled to an offer of a services plan. The school responsible for offering this is *not* the home school but the school district where the private school is located.

The services plan will offer services, say where they are located, and if needed, provide transportation for your child to and from the services.

Children in private schools do not receive the same type or amount of special education and related services they would if they were attending a public school.

More information about Private Schools, Services Plans and Unilateral Placements is in the **NOPS**, at 34 **C.F.R.** §§300.37, 300.111, 300.115, 300.129, 300.130, 300.132, 300.134, 300.135, 300.137, 300.138, 300.130, and in the *Commentary*, **FR**, Vol. 71, No. 156, 46541, 46542, 46569, 46577, 46590, 46592, 46670, 46584, 46585-35486 (2006).

If you remember only one thing from this lesson, remember this: placement decisions are made only after the IEP is complete.

Lesson Summary

In this lesson you learned about placements, unilateral placements, services plans, and Least Restrictive Environment. Next, you will learn about Discipline.

LESSON TEN: Behavior and Discipline

> *If adults can't follow the rules 100% of the time, how can we expect a child to do so?* — *Jim Comstock-Galagan*

Discipline, Suspension, and Expulsion

Some people think schools can't discipline a child who has an **IEP**. That is not true. A school can discipline any child – even one with a disability – who does not follow the school code of conduct.

Schools may not punish a child for behavior related to, linked to, or caused by a disability.

All children have school discipline due process rights. Children with disabilities have additional due process rights to prevent unfair punishment based on their disability. Schools must follow these rules when disciplining a child with a disability.

The Ten-Day Rule

In general, a child with a disability cannot be removed from school for more than ten days for behavior related in any way to a disability. The ten days can happen in a row, or they can accumulate during the school year.

Exceptions to the ten-day rule include using or possessing drugs or weapons or causing serious bodily injury. Children who do these things can be immediately removed from school. You will learn more about serious and dangerous behavior later in this lesson.

The ten-day rule does not apply when a child's behavior is different from behaviors that caused earlier school removals. The new removal is not a change of placement.

Before a school can change the placement of a child with a disability because of behavior, it must hold a Manifestation Determination Meeting (MDM). You will learn more about the MDM later in this lesson.

An expulsion is a long-term removal from school. Sadly, in some states, a child can be expelled for an entire school year.

Any student who is expelled is entitled to an expulsion hearing. This is a separate procedure outside of special education and is beyond the scope of this lesson.

Your state's school discipline laws have information about expulsion hearings. You can also call your state's DOE for more details.

Some school student handbooks include information about the Code of Student Conduct, discipline, expulsion, and disciplinary hearings.

If your school says it is expelling your child, you can ask for special education due process hearing. This hearing can be held before, in place of, or after an expulsion hearing. It can also be held after you receive an expulsion hearing decision.

A special education discipline due process hearing is usually an Expedited Hearing. You will learn more about Expedited Hearings in Lesson Eleven.

Children who have never been evaluated or found eligible for special education may have some due process rights. These rights come into play if your school knew or should have known your child had a disability.

Your school knew or should have known about your child's disability if any one of the following is true:

☞ You asked in writing for an evaluation.

☞ In writing, you told someone you believed your child has a disability.

☞ Someone at school said they thought your child might have a disability.

More information about Discipline, Due Process, Alternative Educational Settings, the ten-day rule, and protections for children not eligible for special education is in the **NOPS**, at 34 **C.F.R.** §§300.530, 300.531, 300.533, 300.534, and in the *Commentary*, FR, Vol. 71, No. 156, 46713 – 46722 (2006).

Weapons, Drugs, Serious Bodily Injury

School can immediately remove a child to an Interim Alternative Educational Setting (IAES) for serious or dangerous behavior.

This includes using or possessing a weapon, using or possessing illegal drugs or controlled substances at school, on school grounds, at a school activity, or causing serious bodily injury.

More information about Weapons, Drugs, and Serious Bodily Injury is at 34 C.F.R. §300.530(g) and (i), and in the *Commentary*, FR, Vol. 71, No. 156, 46628 – 46629, 46722, 46749 – 46750 (2006).

Interim Alternative Educational Settings

Schools can keep a child in an Interim Alternative Educational Setting (IAES) for up to ten school days for serious or dangerous behavior. Once a school places a child in an **IAES**, they can keep them there for up to 45 school days even if the behavior is linked to a disability.

More information about Interim Alternative Educational Settings is in the **NOPS**, at 34 **C.F.R.** §300.530(b)(1), 300.531, 300.532, 300.533, and in the *Commentary*, FR, Vol. 71, No. 156, 46713 – 46726, 46728, 46749 – 46752 (2006).

Manifestation Determination Meeting

A school must hold an **MDM** before it can change a child's placement for disciplinary reasons. Members of the **IEP** team are included in the **MDM** team. Parents are members of both teams.

The **MDM** team looks at the child's current behavior, history of conduct, the disability, and any existing **FBA** and **BIP**.

The **MDM** team decides whether the school followed the child's **IEP**. If it did not, the school can't change the child's placement.

Next, the **MDM** team decides if the child's behavior is related to the disability on a case-by-case basis. The **IEP** is the key document the **MDM** team uses when making this decision.

Suppose the **IEP** says a child can become aggressive. If the incident involves aggression, the behavior is related to the disability. The school cannot remove the child for more than ten days.

Unless the **MDM** team agrees otherwise, when the behavior is related to the disability, the school must return the child to the previous placement. If a Functional Behavioral Analysis (FBA) has not been done, the school should perform one without delay.

When the school completes the FBA, the results are used to design and implement a Behavior Intervention Plan (BIP).

If the child had a BIP when engaging in the behavior, the IEP team should review and revise it. An appropriate BIP is supposed to eliminate or prevent behavior that interferes with educational performance.

Suppose the MDM team decides the behavior is not related to the disability. In that case, the school can suspend, expel, or exclude the child for up to 45 days.

The child must continue to receive all IEP services and have a chance to progress toward the IEP goals during the exclusion.

If you disagree with an MDM team decision, you can file a Due Process Complaint and ask for an expedited due process hearing.

You will learn more about expedited hearings in Lesson Eleven.

More information about Manifestation Determination Meetings is in the NOPS, at 34 C.F.R. §§300.530(e) and (f), 300.532, 300.533 and in the *Commentary*, FR, Vol. 71, No. 156, 36546, 46579, 46692, 46713 – 46716, 46718 – 46729, 46748 – 46749, 46798 (2006).

Disciplinary Change of Placement

A change of placement is a suspension of more than ten cumulative days. If a school suspends a child for more than ten school days during the school year, it must do something to try to keep the behavior from happening again.

Schools have many options to prevent behaviors from interfering with a child's education. The following is a partial list of things schools can do.

- ☞ Use positive behavior interventions.
- ☞ Provide support services and modifications.
- ☞ Perform a new **FBA** or update an existing one.
- ☞ Develop a new **BIP** or review and revise an existing one.

More information about Disciplinary Changes of Placement is in the **NOPS**, at 34 **C.F.R.** §§300.530, 300.531, 300.532, 300.533, 300.536, and Commentary FR, Vol. 71, No. 156, 46719 – 46723, 46728 (2006).

Functional Behavioral Assessment

All behavior is a form of communication. A child with communication disabilities cannot always express their wants and needs. Often this makes them frustrated and angry. These emotions can turn into aggressive behavior.

An **FBA** has several purposes. The first is to look for the reason (trigger or antecedent) that causes a child to behave in a certain way.

Schools can employ trained behavior analysts to find out what triggers a child's behavior. Once this is known, the **BIP** can include strategies to avoid the activity that triggers the behavior.

Next, the **FBA** tries to find out how the child is rewarded for engaging in the behavior.

For example, if the purpose of the behavior is to avoid an environment or setting, removing a child may be a reward.

An **FBA** must find out why a child behaves a certain way and see what he or she gets out of it.

Finding triggers and rewards allows the **IEP** team to place strategies in the **BIP** to stop the behavior or replace it with an acceptable one.

If you disagree with an FBA, you can ask for an independent FBA at school expense.

More information about Functional Behavioral Assessments is at 34 C.F.R. §§300.34(a)(10)(iii) and (vi), 300.530(d)(ii) and in the *Commentary*, FR, Vol. 71, No. 156, 46575, 46683 (2006).

Behavior Intervention Plans

When the FBA is completed, the IEP team will meet to develop a BIP. This plan should include all the strategies, supports, and services to meet your child's behavioral needs.

Services that may decrease negative behavior can include speech/language therapy, social skills training, school social work services, or therapeutic counseling. The IDEA strongly encourages schools to include positive behavioral interventions in the BIP.

The Plan should include a specific date when the team expects the behavior to change or stop. If the child's behavior does not improve by that time, the team should update the FBA or review and revise the BIP.

Unfortunately, The IDEA does not say when schools must do an FBA or modify an existing BIP when a child is removed for disciplinary reasons.

A child's history is the best predictor of future behavior problems. Don't wait for a crisis. Be proactive and ask for an FBA and a BIP.

If your child's BIP does not improve behavior, it is not working. You can ask for a new FBA or review and revision of the BIP.

Best practice is to include the BIP in the IEP. The IDEA does not require this, but your state's law may.

If your child's BIP is a separate document from the IEP, school staff must have "access" to it. Never assume that having "access" to a BIP means staff will actually read it. You may want to consider giving copies of your child's BIP to all school staff who work with your child.

Under the IDEA, an evaluation or a reevaluation does not automatically include an FBA. Your state's law may require it.

A child must be evaluated in all areas of the suspected disability. It makes sense that if a child's behavior or emotional status has an adverse effect on educational performance, an FIE would include an FBA. Don't assume this will happen even if your state law requires it.

More information about BIP's and Positive Behavioral Interventions is at 34 C.F.R. §300.324(a)(3)(i), and in the Commentary, FR, Vol. 71, No. 156, 46629, 46642 – 46643, 46569, 46683, 46716, 46720 – 46721, (2006).

In 2009, the U.S. Department of Education developed a special education school discipline guide: Questions and Answers on Discipline Procedures. The Appendix includes a link to this document.

If you remember only one thing from this lesson, please remember this: your school cannot punish your child for a behavior that is connected in any way to a disability.

Lesson Summary

In this lesson, you learned about Discipline, Functional Behavioral Assessments, and Behavior Intervention Plans. Next, you will learn about Due Process and Alternative Dispute Resolution.

LESSON ELEVEN:

Due Process and

Alternative Dispute Resolution

> *Bullfight critics ranked in rows crowd the enormous plaza full.*
> *There is only one who knows, and that is the one who fights the bull.*
> *- Inscription on the grave of Dorminguez Ortez*

Due Process

You and your child have many due process rights. It would take an entire book to tell you about all of these rights. In this lesson, you will learn about the most crucial due process topics. You will want to continue learning about all the other due process rights this book does not cover.

The term "due process" comes from the Fifth and Fourteenth Amendments of the U.S. Constitution. The Fifth Amendment says no one shall be "deprived of life, liberty or property without due process of law."

The Fourteenth Amendment is the "Due Process Clause." It says, "No State shall make or enforce any law which shall abridge the privileges or immunities of citizens of the United States; nor shall any State deprive any person of life, liberty, or property, without due process of law; nor deny to any person within its jurisdiction the equal protection of the laws."

What do these Amendments mean? Before a government agency can make a decision, act, or refuse to act in any way that affects your or your child's rights, it must give you a way to challenge its decision or actions.

Public schools are government agencies. As government agencies, schools must give you and your child a right to due process, i.e., the right to challenge decisions.

Schools must follow specific procedures before acting or refusing to act in any way that affects your rights or your child's rights. These procedures ensure you and your child have access to a fair legal process.

Your rights as a parent are separate from your child's due process rights. *Winkelman v Parma*

City School District, 127 **S.Ct.** 1994, 167 **L.Ed.2d** 904 (2007).

Alternative Dispute Resolution

Let's talk first about Alternative Dispute Resolution (ADR). Several methods of ADR are available for resolving special education disagreements.

ADR includes "procedures and processes that States have found to be effective in resolving disputes quickly and effectively." ADR does not include the dispute resolution processes required by the IDEA or its regulations. The *Commentary*, FR Vol. 71, No. 156, 46604 (2006).

Mediation

In 1997, Congress added mediation to the IDEA as an added option for parents and schools to resolve special education disagreements.

Mediation is less adversarial and less formal than due process hearings. Plus, it is free to families and schools. Mediation costs only a day of your time.

Mediation is voluntary. You and your school must agree to use mediation. It cannot delay or deny your right to a due process hearing.

You can use mediation in place of a due process hearing. If you have already filed for a hearing, you can use mediation. You can even ask for mediation during your hearing.

If you and your school agree to mediate but fail to settle the dispute, you can still file for a due process hearing.

You and your school can agree to use mediation in place of a resolution meeting. You will learn more about resolution meetings later in this Lesson.

When you and your school agree to use mediation, your state DOE assigns a trained, impartial mediator. This person has no interest in the dispute or the results of the mediation. The mediator makes all arrangements for the mediation, including setting up a convenient time and place for both parties.

Mediators do not make decisions about disagreements between you and the school. The role of a mediator is to act as a facilitator and help you and the school find a way to resolve the dispute.

You should not expect mediation to give you a perfect result. If you and your school agree, neither of you will likely get everything you want.

But mediators are skilled in helping people find solutions to problems in ways that avoid the formal hearing process.

You do not have to resolve all disagreements at mediation. Any issues you can resolve will be formalized by the mediator into a written agreement. The agreement is legally binding as soon as you and the school sign it. A court can order either party to comply with the agreement.

Before you sign a mediation agreement, make sure: (1) It includes everything to which you and the school agreed; and (2) You get a signed copy of the agreement before leaving the mediation session. Do not leave the room without a copy of the agreement.

All discussions and the mediation agreement are confidential. Neither you nor the school can use anything said or written down during mediation in any future legal proceedings.

More information about Mediation is in the **NOPS**, at 34 **C.F.R.** §§300.152(a)(3)(ii), 300.506, 300.510 and in the *Commentary*, **FR**, Vol. 71, **No.** 156, 46601 - 46605, 46624, 46633-46634, 46640, 46661, 46671, 46682, 46694 - 46696, 46700, 46702 - 46703, 46708 - 46709, 46721, 46725, 46730 (2006).

IDEA Due Process Hearings

In 1975, Congress pictured due process hearings as an informal way to resolve problems between parents and schools.

Today, many due process hearings are complex legal proceedings. A few have lasted longer than a murder trial!

In a due process hearing, an **IHO** or an **ALJ** makes decisions usually made by the **IEP** team.

The **IHO** or **ALJ**'s ruling will be based on documents and testimony that each side presents during the hearing.

More information about IHOs and ALJs is at 34 C.F.R. §300.511 and in the *Commentary*, FR, Vol. 71, No. 156, and due process hearings at 34 C.F.R. §300.511, 300.512, 300.513, 300.514, 300.515, 300.516, 300.517, 300.518 and in the *Commentary*, Vol. 71, No. 156, 46601,46604 – 46607, 46661, 46682, 46698, 46704 – 46708, 46723 – 46724, 46726, 46746, and 46748 (2006).

Statute of Limitations

Your state law controls how far back in time you can go when you file for a due process hearing. This is called the "statute of limitations."

The IDEA statute of limitations is two years from the time you knew or should have known about your hearing issues. Your state law may have a different statute of limitations.

Only a few exceptions allow you to go back further than your state's statute of limitations. 34 C.F.R. §300.511(e) and (f).

The NOPS should have Information about your state's statute of limitations, or you can call your state's DOE for more details.

Unless your state law says otherwise, the party that asked for the hearing has the "burden of proof." *Schaffer v. Weast*, 546 US 49 (2005). This means whoever filed the due process complaint must prove its case to the IHO or ALJ. Under the best of circumstances, this can be an uphill battle for most parents.

Due Process Complaints

A due process hearing begins with the filing of a due process complaint. Most hearing requests are filed by parents.

Due process complaints are filed for issues that involve eligibility, evaluations, placement, or whether a child is not receiving **FAPE**. Due process complaints often include several sub-issues.

A due process complaint must include specific information about your child. It must summarize the disagreement, the relevant facts, and a proposed solution to the problem.

Each state has a model due process complaint form. Your **DOE** may post this form on its website. If you cannot find one on the website, call and ask for one to be sent to you.

You don't have to use the model complaint form. By using it, your complaint is more likely to include all the necessary information and helps avoid a Notice of Insufficiency. You will learn about this Notice next.

More information about due process complaints is in the **NOPS** and model due process complaint forms is at 34 **C.F.R.** §300.509 and in the *Commentary*, Vol. 71, **No.** 156, 46699 – 46700 (2006).

Notice of Insufficiency

The process for filing a due process complaint can be complex. A complaint *must* include several things. If it does not include this information, the school can file a Notice of Insufficiency.

The **IHO** or **ALJ** will review the Notice and decide if your complaint has all the required information. Within five days, the **IHO** or **ALJ** will send you and the school an order saying whether the complaint is sufficient.

If your complaint is insufficient, the **IHO** or **ALJ** will say what is missing and give you a chance to amend it. You will learn more about amending your complaint next.

More information about Sufficiency Notices is at 34 C.F.R. §300.508(d) and in the *Commentary*, Vol. 71, No. 156, 46698 - 46700, 46704, 46725 - 46726, (2006).

Amending a Complaint

The IHO or ALJ can allow you to amend your complaint, or you and the school can agree to an amendment.

Amending a complaint starts the hearing timelines over again. If the parents filed the due process complaint, they must also go to another resolution meeting.

More information about amending a due process complaint is at 34 C.F.R. §§300.508(d)(3) and (4) and in the Commentary, FR Vol. 71, No. 156, 46699 (2006).

The Resolution Period

In 2004, Congress added a 30-day resolution period to the due process procedures of the IDEA. During this period, parents who file for a hearing must attend a Resolution Meeting. Refusing to go to the meeting may allow the IHO or ALJ to dismiss the hearing.

The purpose of a resolution meeting is to give schools a chance to resolve the disagreement before the hearing begins. Schools that file for hearings do not have to go to Resolution Meetings.

A Resolution Meeting must take place within fifteen days from the filing of the due process complaint is filed. If your school doesn't schedule a Resolution Meeting, you can ask the IHO or ALJ to allow your hearing to begin.

You and your school can agree to waive a Resolution Meeting or to use mediation instead. The 45-day hearing timeline doesn't start until (1) you go to the Resolution Meeting, (2) you and the school agree to waive the meeting, or (3) after mediation takes place when you and the school agree to use mediation instead of a resolution meeting.

You can invite others with knowledge or expertise about your child to go to the Resolution Meeting. If your attorney attends, the school can send its attorney, too.

If you and your school can solve any of the issues at the Resolution Meeting, you will be asked to sign a written agreement. You and the school have three business days to cancel the agreement. If neither party cancels, the agreement is legally binding. A court can order you or your school to comply with its terms.

You need to know that Resolution Meeting statements and agreements are not confidential. Anything you say, do, or agree to during a Resolution Meeting can be used later in a hearing or court proceeding.

More information about Resolution Meetings is in the **NOPS**, at 34 C.F.R. §§300.510, 300.532(c)(3), 300.537, and in the *Commentary*, FR, Vol. 71, No. 156, 46545, 46694, 46696, 46697, 46698, 46700 – 46704, (2006), and *Letter to Anderson*, **OSEP** (2010). *See also*: S. Rpt. No. 108-185, p. 38 and H. Rpt. No. 108-77, p. 114.

Table 3 compares Resolution Meetings and Mediation.

Table 3

COMPARISON OF MEDIATION AND RESOLUTION MEETINGS	
Mediation	Resolution Meeting
Voluntary.	Mandatory when parents file for hearings.
Facilitated by a trained, impartial mediator.	No impartial person guides the process.
Mediation and mediation agreements are confidential.	Resolution meetings and agreements are not confidential
Signed mediation agreements are legally binding.	Legally binding if neither party cancels within three business days.

Parents may ask others to come to mediation or a resolution meeting

Hearings: The Good, The Bad, The Ugly

Special education due process hearings are based on an adversarial process. They can be ugly, complicated, lengthy, and costly. Often both sides are polarized before the Due Process Complaint is filed.

Without access to a hearing, parents would have no legal way to settle disagreements with their schools. While they may be painful to schools and parents, hearings are a necessary and essential part of special education.

Consulting with an experienced parent attorney may help you decide whether a hearing is suitable for your family. The attorney may be able to suggest ways to resolve disagreements short of a due process hearing.

Working with a parent attorney may also help with damage control. They are usually skilled negotiators and may be able to settle disputes before the hearing begins. Many try to keep you out of the middle of the fray.

As you weigh the pros and cons of a hearing, you should consider some important things. How much will the hearing cost? How long will it last? What will be the other costs to your family besides money?

Hearings are physically, mentally, psychologically, and emotionally exhausting. A hearing can go on for weeks. Some go on for months. The stress can wear down the strongest parents. You must consider these as well as the monetary costs to you and your family.

If your attorney charges a fee, you should discuss the possibility you can recover what you pay. You should also ask what will have to happen for you to do so.

Most hearings require expert witnesses. You will have to budget the amount you pay them to evaluate your child and testify at the hearing.

You may have to take time off work to attend the hearing. There may also be childcare costs during the hearing.

You must decide whether your hearing will be open or closed to the public. Will you want your child to attend and/or testify?

If you live in a state that allows it, will a lay advocate represent you? If so, what do they charge?

Do any experienced parent attorneys practice near you? Will you represent your own child? You will learn about these options later in this lesson.

Appealing a Hearing Decision

You can appeal a decision if you lose at a hearing. In a "one-tier state," you appeal to a state or federal court. In a "two-tier state," you appeal to a panel or an appeals officer before you can file in court.

You can't appeal a decision just because you are unhappy with it or don't like it. You must have a legal reason to appeal. An attorney can explain this in more detail.

More information about appealing hearing decisions is at 34 C.F.R. §§300.514, 300.515, 300.516 and in the Commentary, Vol. 71, No. 156, 46707 (2006).

Stay-Put

Generally, during a hearing and appeal, the child stays in the educational placement he or she was in when the hearing was filed. This is called "stay put."

If the dispute is about an initial evaluation, Stay put does not apply. Your child is not yet eligible for special education.

Stay put does not always apply if a hearing is filed because of a disciplinary change of placement.

More information about Stay Put is in the NOPS, at 34 C.F.R. §300.518, and in the Commentary, Vol. 71, No. 156, 46682, 46709, 46710 46726 (2006).

An Attorney, a Lay Advocate, or Pro Se?

Parents must make the critical decision of who to hire to represent their child during a hearing. You can use an attorney, a lay advocate, in states that allow it, or you can represent your child on your own.

You can use a lay advocate only in states that allow one to practice law in the area of special education. In some states, this is not permitted and may be considered the Unauthorized Practice of Law (UPL).

Other states allow non-attorney advocates or lay advocates to represent parents in hearings, but they cannot charge a fee.

If you live in a state that allows lay advocates to represent a child and charge fees, you may not be able to recover anything you pay.

Who to choose is an important business decision. You must interview the advocate carefully. It is wise to get references from parents they have represented!

Most lay advocates conduct themselves ethically. They honestly want to help families. Many are parents who became advocates because they were successful in getting services for their own children.

Unlike attorneys, most states do not regulate special education lay advocates. They have no formal, required Code of Ethics and Professional Responsibilities. No oversight or disciplinary board supervises their practice.

In addition to being held to no legal or ethical standards, there is no required level of training, experience, or education. Almost everywhere, anyone can say they are a special education advocate.

At the time this book was written, there were few formal advocacy training programs. Only two were affiliated with universities. None provided a certification or licensure. Most offered a certificate of attendance.

Because no standards, licensure, or certification exist, parents must choose a lay advocate with care. It is genuinely *caveat emptor*, or "Let the buyer beware."

Many lay advocates are highly trained, well educated, competent, and accomplished. Some can represent parents at due process hearings almost as well as an attorney. They may be more proficient than a general practice attorney who has no experience with special education law.

You must weigh the pros and cons of using a lay advocate. Be aware of the benefits and risks and choose carefully.

You can find information about lay advocate representation by reading your state **NOPS**, calling your state **DOE**, or in the Commentary, FR, Vol. 71, No. 156, 46699, (2006).

Consulting with an experienced parent attorney or two is a good idea before choosing who to represent your child. Never assume you can't afford one unless you have talked to at least two attorneys.

Some parent attorneys offer free initial consultations. Even if you must pay for a consultation, the advice you get may save you money and grief in the long run.

Some attorneys have payment plans, sliding scales or can refer you to low-cost legal services.

You may represent yourself and your child at a hearing. *Pro se* parents are often at a serious disadvantage.

They must deal with their emotions, often without the legal knowledge and skill needed to successfully represent their child. Even parents who are lawyers learn quite quickly how difficult it is to represent their own child.

Research shows when parents represent their own child, the outcome is often dismal. *See,* Are the Outcomes of Hearing (and

Review) Officer Decisions Different for Pro Se and Represented Parents, Zirkel, P., *Journal of the National Association of the Administrative Law Judiciary*, 34, 265–282.

If you are thinking about being a *pro se* parent, remember that most schools are represented by one or more attorneys. The IHO or ALJ is also usually an attorney.

Representing your own child means you are outnumbered, outmanned, and outgunned before the hearing even begins!

Recovering Attorneys' Fees

If you win or prevail at your hearing, you may be able to recover your attorneys' fees. You may have to go to court to do so.

Your school may try to recover its attorneys' fees from you, your advocate, or your attorney if you file a frivolous, unreasonable, or without foundation due process complaint.

If you file for a hearing to harass your school, it may try to recover its attorneys' fees from you, your attorney, or your lay advocate.

The same is true if you unnecessarily delay or needlessly increase the cost of litigation.

You shouldn't worry about having to pay for a school's legal costs if you have a genuine dispute with your school. On the rare occasions where a school has been successful in recovering its fees, the actions of the parent, the advocate, or the attorney were particularly egregious.

More information about attorney's fees is at 34 C.F.R. §§300.504(c)(13), 300.517 and in the *Commentary*, FR, Vol. 71, No. 156, 46708 – 46709, 46748 (2006)

Expedited Due Process Hearings

In Lesson Ten, you learned a little about expedited hearings for disagreements about a change of placement because of a child's behavior.

Schools can ask for an expedited hearing if a child poses a danger to himself or herself or to others.

An expedited due process hearing shortens the timelines for the hearing and the decision. Unless your state has a different timeline, the hearing must be held within 20 school days from when the due process complaint is filed.

The IHO or ALJ must decide the case within 10 school days from when the hearing ends. The same appeal rights apply as in a non-expedited due process hearing.

More information about expedited hearings is in the NOPS, at 34 C.F.R. §300.532, and in the

Commentary at FR, Vol. 71, No. 156, 46715, 46719 – 46720, 46724 – 46726, (2006)

Section 504 Hearings and Local Grievance Procedures

Section 504 also gives parents the right to an impartial due process hearing and an appeal of the hearing decision. Parents can be represented by an attorney. Whether a lay advocate can represent a parent is decided by state law.

Section 504 provides little guidance on the conduct of due process hearings. Schools set up the procedures, hire the hearing officer, and make all the arrangements. Section 504 hearings can look much different than IDEA hearings.

Section 504 also gives parents a local grievance procedure. Schools must adopt a procedure that has "appropriate due process standards" for the "prompt and equitable resolution of complaints."

If you disagree with the results of a grievance decision, you can appeal by filing an **OCR** complaint. The complaint must be filed within 50 calendar days from the time you get the decision.

More information about Section 504 Hearings and Grievance Procedures is at 34 **C.F.R.** §§104.7, 104.8, and 104.36.

FERPA Hearings

Suppose you believe your child's records are inaccurate, misleading, or violate your or your child's privacy, and your school refuses to change them. In that case, you have a right to ask for a hearing.

If the **IHO** rules against you, you can place a statement in the records saying you disagree with the hearing decision.

Your school must keep this statement in your child's records for as long as it keeps them. It must also release the statement anytime it releases the part of your child's records with which you disagreed.

More information about **FERPA** hearings is at 34 **C.F.R.** §99.20 – 99.22.

If you remember only one thing from this lesson, please remember this: Nothing in a resolution meeting is confidential. Anything can be used later as evidence in a hearing or court proceeding.

Lesson Summary

In this lesson, you have learned about due process, complaints and hearings under the **IDEA**, Section 504, and **FERPA**.

Congratulations! You have completed all Eleven Lessons!

Conclusion

The best ending for this book is to remind you what Congress said when it enacted the Individuals with Disabilities Education Act:

Disability is a natural part of the human experience and in no way diminishes the right of individuals to participate in or contribute to society. Improving educational results for children with disabilities is an essential element of our national policy of ensuring equality of opportunity, full participation, independent living, and economic self-sufficiency for individuals with disabilities. – 20 U.S.C. §1400(c)

Go forth and do good work for the children!

Definitions

The following definitions are in the IDEA Regulations. Check your state's education and special education law to see if they include any additional definitions.

Assistive Technology service: Any service that directly assists a child with a disability in finding, acquiring, or using an assistive technology device. The term includes evaluations, purchasing, lending, or otherwise providing the device, selecting, designing, fitting, customizing, adapting, applying, maintaining, repairing, or replacing devices. 34 C.F.R. §300.5

At no cost: All specially designed instruction is provided free. This does not include incidental fees schools typically charge to all students or their parents as part of the regular education program. 34 C.F.R. §300.39 (b)(1)

Business Day: Monday through Friday, except for Federal and State holidays (unless holidays are expressly included in the designation of business day). 34 C.F.R. §300.11 (b)

Child with a disability: A child who has been evaluated (in accordance with the IDEA) as having one of the listed impairments and who needs special education and related services. 34 C.F.R. §300.8 (This section also defines the characteristics of each listed impairment).

Consent: The parent has been fully informed of all relevant information to the activity for which consent is being sought, in his or her own native language or other mode of communication, the parent understands and agrees in writing to the activity for which their consent is being sought, and the parent knows they can revoke their consent at any time. 34 C.F.R. §300.9

Day: Calendar Day unless otherwise indicated as business day or school day. 34 C.F.R. §300.11 (a) (See definitions for "school day" and "business day")

Evaluation: Procedures used to decide whether a child has a disability and the nature and extent of the special education and related services the child needs. 34 C.F.R. §300.15

Free Appropriate Public Education: Special education and related services, provided at public expense, under public supervision and direction, and without charge, that meets the standards of the State Educational Agency and the IDEA requirements, including preschool, elementary or secondary school education in the state involved, and that are provided in conformity with an IEP that meets the IDEA requirements. 34 C.F.R. §300.17

Individualized Education Plan/Program: A written statement for a child with a disability that is developed, reviewed, and revised in accordance with IDEA. 34 C.F.R. §300.22

IEP Team: A group of individuals responsible for developing, reviewing, or revising a child's IEP. At a minimum, the IEP TEAM includes (1) the parents; (2) a regular education teacher, if the child is, or may be, participating in the regular education environment; (3) a special education teacher; (4) a representative of the public agency who is qualified to provide, or supervise the provision of, specially designed instruction to meet the unique needs of children with disabilities and who is knowledgeable about the general education curriculum, and the availability of resources; (5) If the child has been evaluated, someone who can interpret the instructional implications of the evaluation results; (6) Other individuals at the discretion of the parent or the school who have knowledge or special expertise regarding the child, including related services personnel as appropriate; (7) When appropriate, the child. 34 C.F.R. §300.23, 34 C.F.R. §300.321

Parent: A biological or adoptive parent, a foster parent (unless the state prohibits a foster parent from acting as a parent), a guardian authorized to act as the parent, or authorized to make educational decisions for the child. 34 C.F.R. §300.30

Personally identifiable information: The child's name, the child's parent's or other family member's name, the child's address, personal identifiers, like social security numbers or student numbers, or a list of personal characteristics or other information that makes it possible to identify the child with reasonable certainty. 34 C.F.R. §300.32

Physical education: The development of physical and motor fitness, fundamental motor skills and patterns, and skills in aquatics, dance, and individual and group games and sports, including intramural and lifetime sports, and includes special physical education, adapted physical education, movement education, and motor development. 34 C.F.R. §300.39(b)(2), 34 C.F.R. §300.108

Related Services: Transportation and such developmental, corrective, and other supportive services required to assist a child with a disability to benefit from special education. These include speech-language pathology and audiology services, interpreting services, psychological services, physical and occupational therapy, recreation, including therapeutic recreation, early identification and assessment of disabilities in children, counseling services, including rehabilitation counseling, orientation and mobility services, and medical services for diagnostic or evaluation purposes, school health services, school nurse services, social work services in schools, and parent counseling and training. This section also includes definitions of the listed related services. 34 C.F.R. §300.34

School Day: Any day, including a partial day that children attend school for instructional purposes. School day has the same meaning for all children in school, including children with and without disabilities. 34 C.F.R. §300.11 (c)(1) and (2)

Special education: Specially designed instruction, at no cost to the parents, to meet the unique needs of a child with a disability. It includes instruction in the classroom, in the home, in hospitals and institutions, and other settings, physical education, speech-language pathology services, or any other related service if the service is considered special education under state standards, travel training, and vocational education. 34 C.F.R. §300.39

Specially designed instruction: Adapting, as appropriate to the child's needs, the content, methodology, or delivery of instruction to address the child's unique needs resulting from the disability, and to ensure access to the general curriculum, so the child can meet the educational standards that apply to all children. 34 C.F.R. §300.39 (3)

Supplementary aids and services: Aids, services, and other supports that are provided in regular education classes, other education-related settings, and in extracurricular and nonacademic settings, to enable children with disabilities to be educated with nondisabled children to the maximum extent appropriate. 34 C.F.R. §300.42

Transition services: A coordinated set of activities that is results-oriented, focused on improving the academic and functional achievement of the child to facilitate movement from school to post-school activities, including postsecondary education, vocational education, integrated employment, continuing and adult education, adult services, independent living, or community participation. Transition services are based on the child's needs, considering the child's strengths, preferences, and interests, and includes instruction, related services, community experiences, the development of employment and other post-school adult living objectives, and if appropriate, acquisition of daily living skills and a functional vocational evaluation. 34 C.F.R §300.43

Travel Training/Orientation and Mobility Services: Providing instruction to children with significant cognitive disabilities and other children who require it, to enable them to develop an awareness of the environment in which they live, and learn the skills necessary to move effectively and safely from place to place within school, in the home, at work, and in the community. 34 C.F.R. §300.34(c)(7) and 34 C.F.R. §300.39(b)(4)

Vocational Education: Organized educational programs that are directly related to the preparation of individuals for paid or unpaid employment, or for additional preparation for a career not requiring a baccalaureate or advanced degree. 34 C.F.R. §300.39(b)(5)

OFFICE FOR CIVIL RIGHTS
U.S. DEPARTMENT OF EDUCATION

Headquarters
400 Maryland Avenue, SW, Washington, DC 20202-1100
Customer Service Hotline #: (800) 421-3481 I Facsimile: (202) 453-6012
TTY#: (800) 877-8339 I Email: OCR@ed.gov IWeb: http://www.ed.gov/ocr

Connecticut, Maine, Massachusetts, New Hampshire, Rhode Island, Vermont Office for Civil Rights, *Boston Office* U.S. Department of Education 8th Floor 5 Post Office Square Boston, MA 02109-3921 Telephone: (617) 289-0111 Facsimile: (617) 289-0150 Email: OCR.Boston@ed.gov	**Illinois, Indiana, Iowa, Minnesota, North Dakota, Wisconsin** Office for Civil Rights, *Chicago Office* U.S. Department of Education John C. Kluczynski Federal Building 230 S. Dearborn Street, 37th Floor Chicago, IL 60604 Telephone: (312) 730-1560 Facsimile: (312) 730-1576 Email: OCR.Chicago@ed.gov
New Jersey, New York, Puerto Rico, Virgin Islands Office for Civil Rights, *New York Office* U. S. Department of Education 32 Old Slip, 26th Floor New York, NY 10005-2500 Telephone: (646) 428-3800 Facsimile: (646) 428-3843 Email: OCR.NewYork@ed.gov	**Michigan, Ohio** Office for Civil Rights, *Cleveland Office* U.S. Department of Education 1350 Euclid Avenue Suite 325 Cleveland, OH 44115 Telephone: (216) 522-4970 Facsimile: (216) 522-2573 Email: OCR.Cleveland@ed.gov
Delaware, Maryland, Kentucky, Pennsylvania, West Virginia Office for Civil Rights, *Philadelphia Office* U.S. Department of Education The Wanamaker Building 100 Penn Square East, Suite 515 Philadelphia, PA 19107-3323 Telephone: (215) 656-8541 Facsimile: (215) 656-8605 Email: OCR.Philadelphia@ed.gov	**Arkansas, Kansas, Missouri, Nebraska, Oklahoma, South Dakota** Office for Civil Rights, *Kansas City Office* U.S. Department of Education One Petticoat Lane 1010 Walnut Street, Suite 320 Kansas City, MO 64106 Telephone: (816) 268-0550 Facsimile: (816) 268-0559 Email: OCR.KansasCity@ed.gov
Alabama, Florida, Georgia, Tennessee Office for Civil Rights, *Atlanta Office* U.S. Department of Education 61 Forsyth Street S.W., Suite 19T10 Atlanta, GA 30303-8927 Telephone: (404) 974-9406 Facsimile: (404) 974-9471 Email: OCR.Atlanta@ed.gov	**Arizona, Colorado, New Mexico, Utah, Wyoming** Office for Civil Rights, *Denver Office* U.S. Department of Education Cesar E. Chavez Memorial Building 1244 Speer Boulevard, Suite 310 Denver, CO 80204-3582 Telephone: (303) 844-5695 Facsimile: (303) 844-4303 Email: OCR.Denver@ed.gov

Louisiana, Mississippi, Texas Office for Civil Rights, *Dallas Office* U.S. Department of Education 1999 Bryan Street, Suite 1620 Dallas, TX 75201-6810 Telephone: (214) 661-9600 Facsimile: (214) 661-9587 Email: OCR.Dallas@ed.gov	California Office for Civil Rights, *San Francisco Office* U.S. Department of Education 50 United Nations Plaza San Francisco, CA 94102 Telephone: (415) 486-5555 Facsimile: (415) 486-5570 Email: OCR.SanFrancisco@ed.gov
North Carolina, South Carolina, Virginia, Washington, D.C. Office for Civil Rights, *District of Columbia Office* U.S. Department of Education 400 Maryland Avenue, S.W. Washington, DC 20202-1475 Telephone: (202) 453-6020 Facsimile: (202) 453-6021 Email: OCR.DC@ed.gov	Alaska, American Samoa, Guam, Hawaii, Idaho, Montana, Nevada, Oregon, Washington, and the Northern Mariana Islands Office for Civil Rights, *Seattle Office* U.S. Department of Education 915 Second Avenue, Room 3310 Seattle, WA 98174-1099 Telephone: (206) 607-1600 Facsimile: (206) 607-1601 Email: OCR.Seattle@ed.gov

Appendix

Publications

Wrightslaw: Special Education Law, Peter W.D. Wright and Pamela Darr Wright

Wrightslaw: From Emotions to Advocacy, Peter W.D. Wright and Pamela Darr Wright

Wrightslaw: All About IEPs, Peter W.D. Wright and Pamela Darr Wright

Wrightslaw: All About Tests and Assessments, Melissa Lee Farrall, Ph.D., Peter W.D. Wright, Esq. and Pamela Darr Wright, MA, MSW

A Guide to Special Education Advocacy, Matthew Cohen, Esq.

The Special Education Battlefield, Andrew Cuddy, Esq.

Your Special Education Rights, Jennifer Laviano and Julie Swanson

Secrets of a Special Education Advocate, Yael Cohen

Do-It-Yourself Special Education Due Process: An Educational Guide, Dorene Philpot, Esq.

I Can't Make This Stuff Up – Special Education Funnies, Foibles & Embarrassments, Dorene Philpot, Esq.

Better IEPs, Barbara Bateman, Esq. and Mary Anne Linden

Writing Measurable Goals and Objectives, Barbara Bateman, Esq. and Cynthia Herr

Student Discipline Rights and Procedures: A Guide for Advocates, The Education Law Center

DVDs

Wrightslaw: Surviving Due Process

Websites

Yellow Pages for Kids, https://www.yellowpagesforkids.com

Wrightslaw: https://www.wrightslaw.com

The Council of Parent Attorneys and Advocates: https://www.copaa.net

U.S. Department of Education, Office of Special Education Programs: https://www2.ed.gov/about/offices/list/osers/osep/index.html

Office of Special Education and Rehabilitation Services: https://www2.ed.gov/about/offices/list/osers/index.html

U.S. Department of Education Office for Civil Rights: https://www2.ed.gov/about/offices/list/ocr/index.html

OCR Policy Letters and clarifications: https://www2.ed.gov/about/offices/list/ocr/publications.html

IDEA Policy Letters and clarifications: https://www2.ed.gov/policy/speced/guid/idea/memosdcltrs/index.html

Centers for Parent Information and Resources (Parent Training and Information Centers): https://www.parentcenterhub.org/

Free Legal Research Tools

Many legal research resources are at Wrightslaw,
https://www.wrightslaw.com/

Search tool for laws, bills, codes, regulations, committee meetings and reports, the Congressional Record, plus much more,
https://www.congress.gov/congressional-record/2021/04/30

Official Digitized Codified Federal Regulations and the Federal Register since 1936, https://www.govinfo.gov/

Search tool for the Federal Register since 1994,
https://www.federalregister.gov/

Electronic Code of Federal Regulations – updated online,
https://www.ecfr.gov

State Law and Regulations: Law Librarians' Society of Washington, DC,
https://www.llsdc.org/

Google Scholar Case law search., https://scholar.google.com

Helpful Documents on Wrightslaw

Complaints: https://www.wrightslaw.com/howey/complaints.tips.pdf

Present Levels of Academic Achievement and Functional Performance:
https://www.wrightslaw.com/howey/iep.functional.perf.htm,
https://www.wrightslaw.com/howey/iep.present.levels.htm

Placement: https://www.wrightslaw.com/howey/10tips.placement.htm

Preparing for IEP Meetings:
https://www.wrightslaw.com/howey/iep.plan.produce.provide.htm,
https://www.wrightslaw.com/howey/iep.mtgs.info.concern.htm

Written Opinions: https://www.wrightslaw.com/howey/written.opinions.htm

US Department of Education:

Questions and Answers on Disciplinary Procedures:

https://www2.ed.gov/policy/speced/guid/idea/discipline-q-a.pdf

Questions and answers for Parents who Place Their Child in Private Schools:

https://sites.ed.gov/idea/files/Private_School_QA_April_2011.pdf

Frequently Asked Questions about Charter Schools:

https://www2.ed.gov/policy/speced/guid/idea/memosdcltrs/faq-idea-charter-school.pdf

Frequently Asked Questions about Hearing, Vision, or Speech Difficulties:

https://www2.ed.gov/about/offices/list/ocr/docs/dcl-faqs-effective-communication-201411.pdf,

https://www2.ed.gov/about/offices/list/ocr/docs/dcl-factsheet-parent-201411.pdf

Fast Facts about Extracurricular Activities:

https://www2.ed.gov/about/offices/list/ocr/letters/colleague-201301-504.pdf,

https://www2.ed.gov/about/offices/list/ocr/docs/dcl-factsheet-201301-504.pdf

Resource Guide to Section 504 in Elementary and Secondary Schools:

https://www2.ed.gov/about/offices/list/ocr/docs/504-resource-guide-201612.pdf

Fact Sheet on Restraint and Seclusion:

https://www2.ed.gov/about/offices/list/ocr/docs/dcl-factsheet-201612-504-restraint-seclusion-ps.pdf

Preventing Racial Discrimination in Special Education:

https://www2.ed.gov/about/offices/list/ocr/letters/colleague-201612-racedisc-special-education.pdf

Parent and Educator Resource Guide to Section 504 in Public Elementary and Secondary Schools:

https://www.wrightslaw.com/law/ocr/sec504.guide.ocr.2016.pdf

Protecting Students with Disabilities:

https://www2.ed.gov/about/offices/list/ocr/504faq.html

Podcasts

Let's Talk Sped Law, parent attorney, Jeffrey L. Forte, Esq.

The Special Ed Files, Jennifer Laviano, Esq. and Julie Swanson

Parental Guidance Podcast with parent attorneys, Catherine M. Michael, Esq. and Carla Loon Leader, Esq.:
https://www.listennotes.com/podcasts/parental-guidance-carla-leader-catherine-9t1UZxj-0gI/

YouTube Channels

Wrightslaw: *https://www.youtube.com/user/wrightslaw*

About the Author

A self-taught reader by age four, Pat's parents enrolled her in kindergarten two weeks after she turned five years old.

From early in elementary school, Pat wondered why she could read better than children several grades above her but could not master basic math facts. One day she would "get" it. The next day it was gone. Six years of tutoring from a licensed teacher did not help. Pat just could not memorize the most basic math facts.

Labeled lazy, unmotivated, and not working up to her ability, Pat finally gave up. She took the easiest high school classes available, majoring in art and business. During high school, it was never in her plans to go to college.

As an adult, Pat quit several jobs because she could not do the required math. She dropped out of three colleges as soon as she learned she had to take a math class. In her mid-forties, she enrolled in her fourth college. On her first day on campus, she asked the college's student services to test her and learned what she had come to suspect was true. She was not lazy; she had Dyscalculia, a form of Dyslexia.

Using a calculator, Pat passed her college math and statistics classes with A's and B's. She knew how to do the math; she just could not do the calculations. She graduated magna cum laude, earning a 3.775-grade point average. To this day, without a calculator, she cannot add, subtract, multiply or divide.

Pat has a B.A. in Paralegal Studies from Saint Mary-of-the-Woods College. She is a member of Lambda Epsilon Chi, an Indiana Registered Paralegal, and an affiliate member of the Indiana Bar and the American Bar Associations. She has been a nationally known Parent Advocate since 1987.

Pat was a founding Board member of the Council of Parent Attorneys and Advocates, a Commissioner on Tippecanoe County's first Human Rights Commission, and past president of Tippecanoe Parents and Professionals for Special Education. Pat was the recipient of the Learning Disabilities Association of Indiana's (LDA-IN) Outstanding Service Award for her commitment and compassion towards students with disabilities.

Pat has authored many articles published on the Wrightslaw website and has been a member of its Speakers Bureau since 2005. From 2010 through 2021, she was a faculty member of the College of William and Mary Law School's annual Institute of Special Education Advocacy in Williamsburg, Virginia.

Pat currently works as a paralegal in the Education Law Division of Connell Michael Kerr Law, LLP. located in Carmel, Indiana.

She works with the firm's Texas, Indiana, Ohio, and Michigan attorneys. Her work includes reviewing education and medical records, issue-spotting, drafting due process complaints and other legal documents, preparing cases for and assisting at hearings, and doing tasks as needed for federal court cases.

Pat lives in the middle of a corn (or bean) field near Odell, Indiana, with her husband, Clark, a retired farmer. She enjoys traveling and playing with her grandchildren and her great-grandchildren.

Made in the USA
Columbia, SC
20 July 2021